Hands Down: A Domestic Violence Treatment Workbook

Sue Binder, LPC, LAC

Domestic Violence Offender Treatment Provider

American Correctional Association
Alexandria, Virginia

Mission of the American Correctional Association
The American Correctional Association provides a professional organization for all individuals and groups, both public and private, that share a common goal of improving the justice system.

American Correctional Association Staff

Gary D. Maynard, President
James A. Gondles, Jr., CAE, Executive Director
Gabriella M. Klatt, Director, Communications and Publications
Harry Wilhelm, Marketing Manager
Alice Heiserman, Manager of Publications and Research
Michael Kelly, Associate Editor
Dana McCoy, Graphics and Production Manager

Production by Capitol Communication Systems, Inc.

Copyright 2007 by the American Correctional Association. All rights reserved. The reproduction, distribution, or inclusion in other publications of materials in this book is prohibited without prior written permission from the American Correctional Association. No part of this book may be reproduced by any electronic means including information storage and retrieval systems without permission in writing from the publisher.

All artwork copyright 2006, Art Behind Bars, "Art-Based Community Service for Inmates"
PO Box 2034, Key West, FL 33045-2034; website: www.artbehindbars.org
Photography by Tony Gregory and Damian Vantriglia; Graphic Layout by Damian Vantriglia

Photographs of Owen and Mzee used with permission from Turtle Pond Publications, New York, New York, Copyright 2006.

Printed in the United States of America by Versa Press, East Peoria, Illinois.

For information on publications and videos available from ACA, contact our worldwide web home page at: www.aca.org

ISBN: 978-1-56991-244-7

This publication may be ordered from:
American Correctional Association
PO Box 201
Annapolis, MD 20701
1-800-222-5646 ext. 0129

Contents

Introduction 1

Chapter 1: Definitions of Domestic Violence 13

Chapter 2: Basic Domestic Violence Issues 33

Chapter 3: Thinking Skills 49

Chapter 4: Communication 61

Chapter 5: Relationships 83

Chapter 6: Anger, Stress, and Domestic Violence 131

Chapter 7: The Role of Substance Abuse 149

Chapter 8: Problem Solving and Conflict Management 159

Chapter 9: Self-Management 169

Conclusion 189

Additional Resources and Reading 191

Introduction

(1 Session)

The program provides you with the opportunity to examine and analyze your own thinking and behavior. This will allow you to make changes in your life and develop healthy relationships. We hope you will discover your own potential through this program and begin to make positive changes, even if you are behind bars.

Objectives

▶ To understand the purpose of the program and how to use this manual

▶ To introduce the facilitator and participants to each other

▶ To establish ground rules for the class

Purpose of the Program

Hands Down: A Domestic Violence Treatment Workbook is designed to help offenders recognize their behaviors—those that have led to problems in intimate relationships. This program covers the basics of domestic violence. This includes discussions of how violent behaviors develop and how to develop new behaviors that are not violent. It also provides assistance within a group setting for learning new methods of dealing with anger. These include controlling feelings and thinking before acting. This program is designed to be used in jails, prisons, boot camps, in juvenile facilities, and in community corrections. Family and criminal courts, hospitals, refugee and victims' services agencies also can use the program to assist in helping you and other men break the cycle of violence.

This program generally runs from twenty-four to thirty-six weeks, but your program may differ. The leader of your group will inform you about the length and times the group will meet. This is a large workbook and your leader will tell you the lessons you are to complete for homework and which ones the group will skip, but which you may wish to work on yourself.

Purpose of the Workbook

This manual provides information about the factors involved in domestic violence. Doing the exercises in each unit should help you to recognize your past behaviors, which have led to current problems. Then, it can help you to develop personal accountability—to take charge of your behavior so the results are not the same as they have been, but are positive and life-affirming both for you and those around you.

The manual has ten sections: Introduction; Definitions of Domestic Violence; Basic Domestic Violence Issues; Thinking Skills; Communication; Relationships; Anger, Stress and Domestic Violence; The Role of Substance Abuse; Problem-Solving and Conflict Management; and Self-Management. The focus is on helping you to develop cognitive skills (thinking behavior). Based on this, you will recognize how your thinking contributes to your abusive behavior. Finally, the goal is for you to develop new skills so that you can change past patterns of behavior.

Why are men targeted? The workbook mainly focuses on male offenders, because men most often are the primary offenders in most domestic violence arrests. Most often, women express their anger and stress differently from men. Also, due to the physical differences between men and women, women are more likely to be injured in a physical fight with a male partner. However, it is important to remember that women do commit domestic violence. Neither gender has a monopoly on violence.

Changing your behavior is possible. By working through the exercises, we hope that individuals who are serious about making changes in their relationships will discover their own potential and make positive changes in their lives and future relationships. The change even can begin behind bars. Men can demonstrate their changed behavior during visitation, by writing letters, by making positive telephone calls, and certainly by displaying their positive attitude in all their activities during the program.

Use of this manual. This manual may be used by individuals or in a group setting. In a group setting, participants can confront each other, encourage each other, and generally share information. This can assist in the growth of all members.

Ground Rules

In a group setting, establishing ground rules from the beginning is vital. For example, each individual must honor confidentiality. This means not revealing or telling others what you have heard about others. You will sign a contract on pages 6-7 that states you understand this idea and will keep to it. The counselor or group leader is bound by confidentiality except for two exceptions—when you threaten to harm another or yourself.

Other group rules include issues of attendance and discharges. Attendance at all classes is necessary to profit from this program. You will not be allowed to continue in the class if you miss too many sessions or repeatedly arrive late. We will discuss these ground rules and by signing the contract, you indicate that you understand them and will go along with them.

Your progress in the program will be judged in the following ways:

- Your attitude toward class and treatment as shown by your upbeat participation in discussions

- Your attendance and punctuality

- Your completion of assignments on time

- Your interaction with the group as shown by positive comments and encouragement of others

- Your not cursing and not using gender, racial, or ethic slurs or putdowns

- Your demonstration of empathy for victims as seen in your comments

- Your displaying less use of controlling behavior

- Your acceptance of personal responsibility for your behavior as shown in your comments and assignments

- Other items as described by your group leader

Victim safety and accountability for your behavior are the main focus of this workbook. The main goal is to avoid creating any more victims—including you. The next goal is for you to demonstrate accountability for your actions. In other words, you must take responsibility for your behavior—both the physical and mental aspects of it. This will require discussion of all parts of your behavior—including things you have done that may have been deviant, unlawful, or nasty. Change is possible. **You can learn to become a different and better person.**

As you progress through the workbook, we hope that your journey will be successful. You will see that you have the ability to make good choices in your life, and to find the joy of a healthy relationship.

"Man Trapped by Ropes of His Own Fate, Wearing a Mask," by BP. Media: Toothpaste, Kool-Aid™ powder, colored pencils, and coffee creamer on recycled cardboard. Courtesy of Art Behind Bars.

Hands Down: A Domestic Violence Treatment Workbook

First Exercise—Introductions

A. In a group setting, select one person in the room you do not know. Spend five minutes interviewing that person. Learn his name and three other things he is willing to share with you (hobbies, marriage, kids, job, or other items). At the end of five minutes, this person will interview you in the same manner. When the instructor, calls for time, you will introduce the other person to the group and he will introduce you. You may use these lines for your notes.

_____
_____
_____
_____
_____
_____
_____
_____
_____
_____

B. What You Hope to Gain from This Class

Write several sentences about what you hope to gain from this class.

_____
_____
_____
_____
_____
_____

Group Contract

Client Agreement to Confidentiality

Generally speaking, information you are provided and which you provide during group sessions is legally confidential. The group leader cannot be forced to disclose information without your permission. However, information can be given to authorities if you are a danger to yourself (suicidal) or to others. If you present a threat to anyone, that information can be revealed. If you threaten any victim, that person and law enforcement will be notified. Everyone should honor the confidentiality of the group, but individuals should understand that the leader cannot guarantee such confidentiality in a group setting.

I also understand that my file may be reviewed from time to time by a supervisor, domestic violence counselor, or consultant with the department of corrections. I agree to this review. Active domestic violence cases will require releases for the victims and notification of victims or the victim's advocate upon discharge. The program operates under the confidentiality regulations of the Health Insurance Portability and Accountability Act of 1996 (HIPAA).

Absences and Tardies

If you are absent more than _____ times, you may be eliminated from the program. Too many tardies also may result in such discharge.

Completions

1. You will be given a completion certificate at the end of the program if you have done all the exercises and participated in the discussion. This means that you have made satisfactory progress, and that you have completed all the requirements of the contract.

2. If you are transferred or move, you will be given credit for the number of classes completed, if you have made successful progress.

3. If you violate the contract or any legal requirements, you will receive an Unsuccessful Discharge.

4. Please add other discharge conditions for your particular program:

_____

_____

Group Expectations

The group leader will discuss his or her expectations with group members. You must comply with the following rules or you may be discharged from the group:

- Confidentiality—no revealing identity of other group members or giving information which could identify them to other people.

- No violence will be tolerated. Violence is grounds for immediate discharge.

- No alcohol or drug use.

- No obscene language.

- No sexist, racial, ethnic or gender, or any derogatory remarks toward others.

- You must demonstrate accountability for your past actions.

- You must not use controlling behaviors.

- Discussions must focus on theme and treatment goals.

Other

_____

_____

I agree to all of the above requirements and agree to provide any Releases of Information to those with whom I agree to share information. I have read the contract and understand it. I am aware that care and treatment in this area of human services is not an exact science. No guarantees have been made that I will magically improve by taking this class, but I will give it my best shot.

_____   _____
Participant's Signature   Date

_____   _____
Leader's Signature   Date

The Hippo and the Tortoise:
A Tale of Respect and Friendship

In 2004, a baby hippopotamus was rescued from the major tsunami in the Indian Ocean. A man named Owen tackled the hippo to the ground. This allowed others to undo the fishing ropes that entangled him. Rescuers named the hippo "Owen". They brought this very frightened animal to Mombasa, Kenya. All other family members of the hippo were lost in the flood. Hippo Owen was brought ashore. He ran to a giant tortoise, Mzee, who was nearby. At first, the tortoise rejected him. The hippo persisted. The tortoise began to return signs of affection. Now, they spend their days together in the pond. At times, Owen nudges Mzee to go for a walk. They seem to enjoy their time together.

The photos of the hippo and the tortoise are real. We thought you would enjoy seeing the positive energy of this unusual relationship. If the baby hippopotamus and the 120-year-old tortoise can get along in a loving manner, maybe you can, too. Perhaps you can consider how well two different species get along. Use their connection to guide your life. Maybe it will lead you to having better relationships with a person important to you. If an interspecies relationship can work, maybe you can get your own relationships to work better, too.

We wrote captions for these pictures. After you finish all the lessons in this course, return to the pictures and add your own captions.

Sometimes you learn about a person by following behind and observing what he or she is doing and not forcing yourself on another. Friendship is important to gain a positive basis for a healthy relationship. Source: Courtesy of Turtle Pond Publications.

Sometimes it is important to learn about each other and try to view things through another's eyes. Women, like the tortoise, can retreat into their shell. They may not be available to you unless you make an effort to be responsible for your own behavior. Source: Courtesy of Turtle Pond Publications.

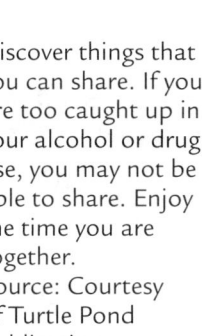

Discover things that you can share. If you are too caught up in your alcohol or drug use, you may not be able to share. Enjoy the time you are together.
Source: Courtesy of Turtle Pond Publications.

The Hippo and the Tortoise

Watch out for each other in a positive way. Having someone to spend time with and share the good and bad times is important. Source: Courtesy of Turtle Pond Publications.

When you are stressed out and angry, you may not have room for affection. Despite different family backgrounds and losses, friendship can grow. Source: Courtesy of Turtle Pond Publications.

When you get rid of your anger, you can enjoy each other's company. There is room for another person in your life. Source: Courtesy of Turtle Pond Publications.

The Hippo and the Tortoise

Do not wreck a good relationship by going back to bad behavior. You are in charge of your behavior.
Source: Courtesy of Turtle Pond Publications.

Chapter 1: Definitions of Domestic Violence

(2–3 Sessions)

Objectives

▶ To define domestic violence

▶ To examine your past violent behavior

▶ To explore power and control issues

▶ To begin the process of developing personal accountability

Accountability

Are you angry about being in a domestic violence class? Do you feel that you do not belong here? Perhaps you are thinking right now: *But I never hit my wife! I never laid a hand on her. It is not fair. The laws are stupid! You can get arrested just for having an argument.*

To a certain extent, you may be right. You may not have hit your partner. The truth is that many men arrested for domestic violence do not believe they have committed a crime.

They seem to think that if they have not struck their partner, then they have not committed domestic violence. You may be thinking the same way. Perhaps you do not realize that violence comes in many forms.

One of the goals of this chapter is to help you learn what behaviors are included in domestic violence. In addition, you will be given information about healthy relationships in which the goal is to treat your partner as an equal. As you begin to examine your own past behavior, you may be able to begin changing your thinking and behavior, so that you can experience stronger and healthier relationships.

Types of Violence

First, what types of domestic violence are there? Domestic violence can be divided into four categories. They include the following:

- Physical abuse
- Sexual abuse
- Verbal abuse
- Emotional or psychological abuse

Physical abuse is quite obvious. It includes striking, slapping, burning a partner, twisting an arm, pulling hair, choking, kicking, pinning her against a wall or the floor, or banging her head. All these are obvious forms of physical abuse. Have you ever shoved your partner? Shoving is a very common form of abuse, one often overlooked by people when they insist they never have had a physical assault with a partner.

Sexual abuse includes rape. Many men do not realize that marital rape is a form of domestic violence. Just because you are married does not give you the right to force your partner to have sex—or to manipulate your partner into having sex. If a spouse, a cohabitating partner, or other intimate partner says "no," that means "no." *Sexual abuse* is forcing someone to perform any sexual act without consent.

However, sexual abuse goes beyond the act of rape or coerced sex. It also includes engaging in sexual harassment or demeaning or offending a person sexually. In other words, it includes emotional or psychological abuse. For example, telling your partner she's a lousy "lay" or telling your friends about her sexual capabilities (especially in front of her) are forms of abuse. Another form of sexual abuse can include using sex as punishment. You are angry at your spouse and refuse to have sex. Perhaps you even sleep on the sofa. You even may refuse sex for days to get even. This, too, is just another form of sexual abuse.

Verbal abuse includes any use of words to control or hurt another person. Have you ever accused your partner of having an affair? How about calling her a "bitch" or "whore" when you are angry? Verbal abuse includes yelling at her, insulting her, making accusations, using sarcasm, threatening to use violence or kill a person or yourself, name-calling, or threatening to hurt the children. Almost everyone has engaged in verbal abuse at some time during a relationship. One of the primary ways that people offend in this area is by name-calling. It is easy to resort to name-calling as a way to "push buttons" when you are angry.

All violence starts with verbal abuse. Then, it moves up to the next level—physical or sexual violence.

Emotional or psychological abuse includes physical, sexual, and verbal abuse. It also falls into its own category. Other behaviors can include: not allowing your partner to have money, not allowing her to go to school or work, isolating her, having unfounded jealousy, withholding sex, criticizing her looks or her thinking, having affairs, spending money recklessly, not working, and/or using alcohol or other drugs. These are just a few of the many ways that people can use emotional abuse against a partner. Have you ever told your partner that she is stupid, dumb, ugly, fat, or a bad mother? Over a period of time, such remarks actually can brainwash a person into believing they are true. This is one way that an insecure man tries to keep his partner with him. However, it rarely works. Your partner will grow tired of such tactics and begin to seek a way out.

Definition of Domestic Violence

Do you now see some of the factors included in domestic violence? Domestic violence is not just hitting your partner. It does not only occur when a person is taken to a hospital with injuries. It also can include damaging the other person's property or hurting a household pet. It includes repetitive and intense behaviors, such as putting the person down, stalking, or harassing. It also can include withholding funds, taking money, and using funds to manipulate or control the other person.

Examine the following definition:

> **Domestic violence is an act in which a perpetrator uses physical, sexual, verbal, or emotional abuse to control, manipulate, coerce, or force a person with whom he has an intimate relationship to do any act against that person's will.**

Exercise 1.1: Types of Abuse I Have Used

1. Review the prior information. Now, list the types of abuse which you have committed in the past against your partner or partners.

_____

_____

_____

_____

_____

2. Draw a line to match the following types of abuse.

A. Physical	. Forced her to have sex
B. Emotional	. Called her a "bitch"
C. Sexual	. Slapped her
D. Verbal	. Accused her of being a bad mom

State definitions of domestic violence. In some states, the definition of domestic violence may include past partners or those with whom a person has had a brief sexual encounter. It may include partners of the same sex. For specific information, consult the laws and standards of your own state. For the purposes of this manual, domestic violence will NOT refer to child or elder abuse.

Intention. A perpetrator does not have to "intend" to harm the other person. This is not part of the definition in this manual. "I didn't intend to" often is used to justify the perpetrator's actions. You may have used the same statement, but it is not a valid excuse. Most offenders do not start the day off by saying, "I'll go home tonight and beat up my wife." Domestic violence is a build up of emotions and stress over a period of time. It occurs due to many factors, which are discussed as you continue through this manual.

Domestic violence is a choice you make.

Exercise 1.2 Reasons for Committing Domestic Violence

Why do you think you committed any act of domestic violence in the past?

_____
_____
_____
_____
_____
_____
_____
_____

Power and Control

Have you ever been afraid of anything? Silly question. All of us have been afraid of something at some time in our lives. Maybe you were afraid when you were standing before the judge waiting to be sentenced. Or, maybe you were afraid when you were face-to-face with someone holding a pistol pointed at you. Whatever your fears, they were real. Fears can overwhelm you, or they can guide you to make good decisions.

Most of your decisions in life are centered around your fears. Think of it. The fear is that we will not succeed in our work. The fear is that we will not succeed, so we do not take a chance. Some people fear that someone they love will die. Others fear that someone we love will leave us.

Think about that last one: *the fear that someone we love will leave us*. Such fear can drive you to do reckless and even criminal acts. It can lead you to rely on power and control methods to force someone to stay with you against her will. That person may stay just because she is afraid.

What makes up power and control tactics?

Power and Control Tactics

Coercion
Threats
Economic abuse
Escape mechanisms
Gender abuse
Intimidation
Isolation
Jealousy
Using children

As we discuss these items, try to recall situations where you have used these tactics. Remember, they are born out of deep fear—often your own insecurities. If you do not feel good about yourself and your relationship, you may be using many power and control tactics to try to force your partner to remain with you. In other words, you are "running scared."

Coercion and Threats. Have you ever tried to convince or force your partner to do what you wanted? Have you refused to listen to her point of view? For example, she wants to go back to school. You refuse. After all, she might meet someone there. She might get smarter than you or make more money. You tell her she's stupid, that she can't make the grades; she's been out of school too long. Besides, how will she get her housework done and care for the children? When she becomes more determined, you threaten to leave if she enrolls. Maybe you even threaten to break her arm. So, she relents.

Exercise 1.3 Use of Coercion or Threats

What other way have you used coercion or threats in the past with a partner? Describe your actions.

_____
_____
_____
_____
_____

Economic Abuse. Some men act as if they are in charge of the finances in the relationship, period. You may have acted the same way. Did your wife have to beg for grocery money? Did you take her money over her protests? Did you spend money without her input? Does she even know how much money is owed, or how much you make? These are important questions. Yet, many people fail to share this important household information with their partners. Why? It boils down to power and control issues.

If you prevent your wife from having a job, if you make her dependent on you for all sources of income, then you have her in your control. If she has to beg for money for the basic necessities, such as hygiene products, something is wrong. A marriage or a relationship should be a partnership. When economic abuse occurs, someone is trying to control the other person through the use of finances.

Just a word of caution. Economic abuse does NOT mean refusing to buy a big-screen television or allowing your partner to max out all the credit cards because you might be accused of controlling her. It does mean jointly talking over family purchases, and it may mean cutting up the credit cards.

Exercise 1.4 Use of Economic Power and Control

Review the financial situation in your past relationships. Write down any times that you may have used economic power and control.

_____

_____

_____

_____

Escape Mechanisms. Escape mechanisms occur whenever you try to justify your behavior. You make excuses for your bad behavior or a poor decision you have made. By doing so, you are attempting to lower your anxiety, tension, or guilt by denying or distorting a stressful situation. Your mind is defending itself from an unpleasant reality by concealing the source of the anxiety from yourself or others.

It happens all the time. For example, you buy a car you can't afford and when you can't make the payments, you say to your friend, "I didn't have a choice. The old one was nickel-and-diming me to death."

Most of the time, escape mechanisms are relatively harmless. However, when used to justify violence, they are not harmless. They can keep you from being honest with yourself. But, more importantly, they get in the way of communicating with the other person and making healthy changes in your behavior.

Some ways in which escape mechanisms are used include:

- Minimizing the abuse
- Denying it happened
- Blaming someone or something else

We will examine each of these mechanisms.

Minimizing. This simply means making something smaller or less important. Perhaps you slap your partner across the face, and she begins to cry. Then, you make light of it. You say, "I didn't hit you that hard. Stop acting like a baby." Or "It wasn't that bad. You're overreacting." You act as if it is not important. You make it less than it really was. Another example of this occurs when a perpetrator is sent for classes and he tells the counselor, "I don't know why I'm here. It was only a verbal argument. I don't beat on my wife." Perhaps he has not struck his wife. Perhaps he only calls her vile names and treats her like a servant. He does not see his behavior as abusive. Or, perhaps he really did physically abuse his wife, but does not want to admit it. So, he tells everyone that it was only a verbal argument, but the cops overreacted.

Another example of minimization occurs when you do not take your partner's concerns seriously. She tells you there is a problem in the relationship. You refuse to acknowledge it. After all, it is not like you hit her with a closed fist. It was just a little shove or a push. What's the big deal? Perhaps she asks if you can go to couple's counseling. You refuse, stating something like, "There's nothing wrong here. It's all in your head."

This is minimization—making it less important than it really is and failing to take full responsibility for your actions. Sometimes, it may be that you simply do not want to believe that you actually abused your partner. More often, you do not want other people to know what you did.

Denying it Happened. This is self-explanatory, also. You just flat out state it never happened. Some men will deny domestic violence happened with the police report sitting right in front of them. Even when confronted with witnesses, the man in denial still will say it never happened. Instead, he will say, "She lied." "The cops lied." "I wasn't even there."

Blaming. This is so common among abusers that it is almost always present when someone comes to treatment. Of course, the first person to blame is the victim. It is all her fault. She started it. She hit first. Maybe you even have said, "She provoked me" or "A man can take only so much." We will examine this idea later in the workbook. For now, consider the idea that no one can provoke us. **You still make a choice of how to act or react. Regardless of provocation, your actions are still your responsibility.**

Secondly, it is common to blame the police. They did not get your side of the story. She's a woman, so naturally, they are siding with her. The laws are stupid and unfair. The cops are out to get you and probably are taking money on the side.

In addition, many people blame the system, a situation, or other people. For example, they blame the "stupid laws," the judge, the court, or your mother-in-law. She's nosey and her advice has caused your wife to accuse you. You blame stress, work, the new baby, or drugs and alcohol. In other words, you shift responsibility for your actions and fail to take responsibility for your own behavior.

Exercise 1.5 Escape Mechanisms or Excuses

1. Think of the escape mechanisms you have used in the past connected with abusive behavior. Make a list below.

_____

_____

_____

_____

2. Now, consider how you should have acted in the situations just listed. What changes could you have made to be totally honest about your behavior?

___
___
___
___
___

Gender Abuse. Gender abuse is also known as *male privilege*. It occurs when a man uses power and control tactics just because he is a man and should be "the head of the household." Sometimes it occurs because men have gotten the message in our culture that they are superior to women. If you have been the one who made all the "big decisions" in the family, without consulting your partner, you may be guilty of this type of abuse. Have you ever said, "That's woman's work" when asked to help with the dishes or the kids? Do you classify chores as belonging to men or women? Do you treat your partner as if she is a servant and order her around?

Exercise 1.6 Gender Abuse

1. Review the idea of gender abuse. Then, note any times that you have used this with a partner.

___
___
___
___
___

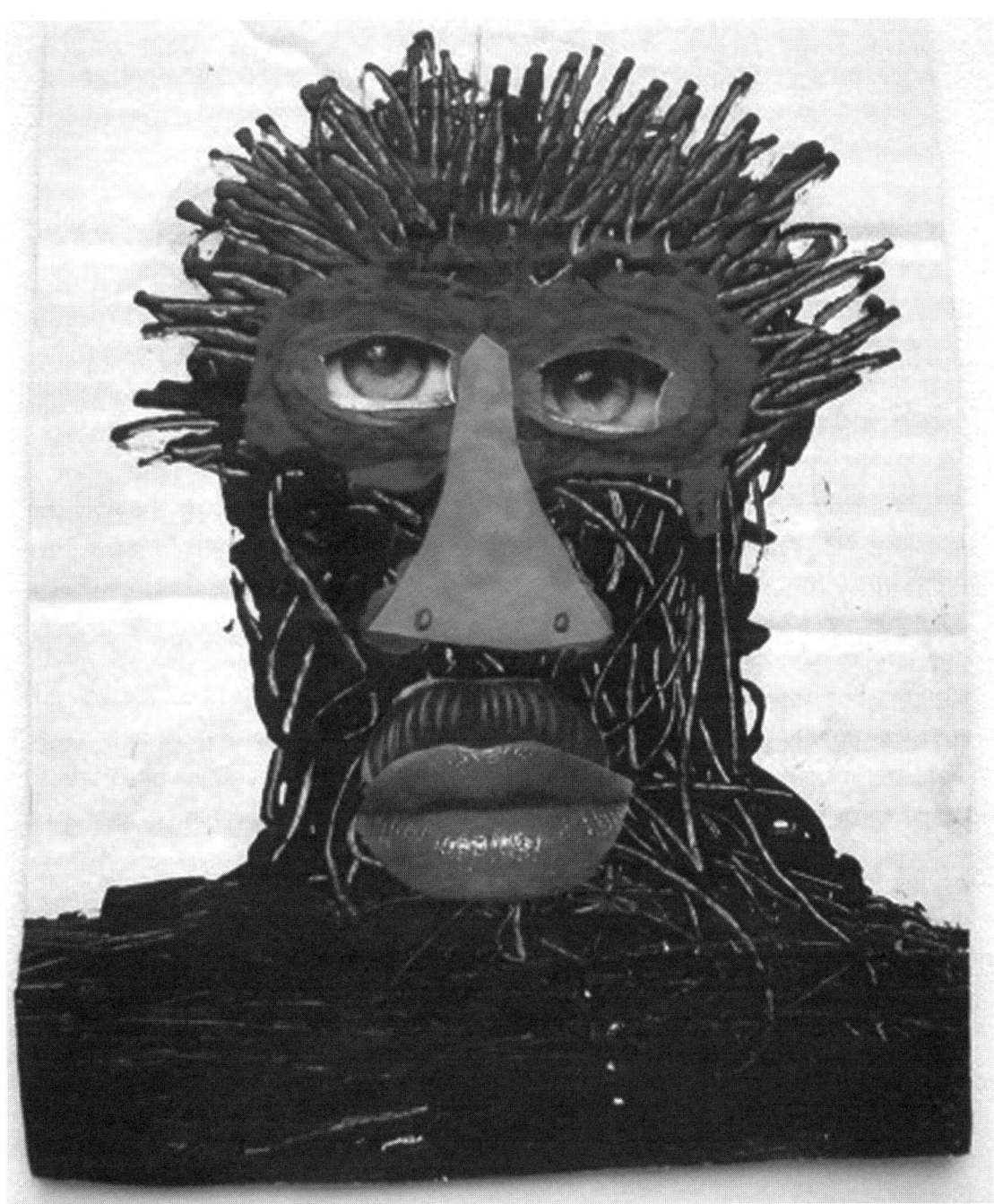

"Rap Star in Heavy Metal World," by BP. Media: Homemade paint, floor wax, toothpaste, coffee creamer, Kool-Aid™ powder, ink, highlighter, and zine cutouts on recycled cardboard. Courtesy of Art Behind Bars.

Intimidation. You are at a party with your girlfriend. You are talking to a couple of friends across the room. You look up and see her talking to a man. She is laughing. In your mind, you think she is flirting with him. You do not have any evidence that she is flirting. You do not know anything about the man or the situation. But, you do not like the idea of her talking with another man. After all, she might get funny ideas. So, when she glances your way, you raise an eyebrow, cock your head just a bit, so your friends do not notice, but she notices. This is not the first time that you have warned her about talking with other men. Then, without another word, she quietly moves away from the man. She knows, just by your look, actions, or gestures that she better not be talking with him. This is one type of intimidation.

But intimidation may include other actions, such as breaking things such as her favorite coffee mug—or just going nuts in the kitchen and breaking up dishes to terrify her. It can include destroying your partner's clothes or other items belonging to her. The message that she gets with this destruction is "This could be your face next time."

You may say, "I didn't mean it that way. I was just angry." But, this is not the way that a victim sees it. It is very fearful when someone starts breaking up household items, especially if those items hold sentimental value.

Another way that people sometimes use intimidation is by displaying weapons, such as waving a gun or threatening their partner with a knife. When a weapon gets involved, the criminal charges may be raised to a felony. But, more important, it is extremely frightening to a victim. That person will probably do what you want her to do because she is scared, but she may lose respect for you. Eventually, you may have destroyed any love she once had for you.

Intimidation also can involve abusing household pets. Your partner has a pet dog, for example, and you are angry at her, so you kick the dog across the room. Now, you have scared her. You have used the animal to manipulate her. Again, this is another form of power and control.

Exercise 1.7 Intimidation

Intimidation can be very subtle. Think of times when you have intimidated a partner in some of the ways listed or in any other ways you can think of. List them.

_____

_____

_____

_____

_____

Isolation. Have you ever told your partner that she could not see her girlfriends anymore? Have you ever told her she could not read a certain book? Have you denied her going to school? Have you ever taken her to the store because she might flirt with one of the checkers if she were alone?

Some of these questions may sound silly to you, but they are not unique. Many abusers isolate their partners in some way. Sometimes they refuse to let them have any outside social activities. Sometimes, they strand them at home with no car, no phone, and no way to get help if there is a domestic incident. Some men have moved their wives to an isolated area, where they have little, if any, outside contact with others.

Exercise 1.8 Isolation

1. Take a few moments and examine your own isolation tactics. Now, write ways in which you have been guilty of this power and control tactic.

_____

_____

_____

_____

_____

Jealousy. In addition, some men will justify their behavior based on jealousy. We will talk about jealousy at greater length later in the workbook, but for now, remember that jealousy generally comes from your own insecurities. If you do not feel good about yourself, then you are going to continually be feeding yourself "bad messages." These messages can include such items as "I'm not a smart as others; my job's lousy; I'm not as handsome as other guys; she probably doesn't love me anymore."

This negative thinking can take over and lead to explosive incidents. Generally, jealousy is unfounded, and it is based on fear. The fear may be that she will find someone else and that you will be rejected. Whatever the reason, jealousy leads to power and control—you try to control your partner's actions, so that she has no choice but to remain with you. You justify this by telling yourself that it is for her own good. Sometimes people show jealousy when they are the one who is cheating. For example, you are having an affair. So, you know that sometimes people do these things. Therefore, you are very concerned that your partner might do the same thing if the opportunity arises. So, you try to prevent her from having an opportunity. You do not trust her.

Exercise 1.9 Jealousy

1. Think back to a time when you were jealous. Describe that time and how you tried to handle it. Also, describe the outcome. Did it work?

_____

_____

_____

_____

Using Children. Imagine you are having an argument with your wife. You are angry over how she has been spending the money. You are on the sofa trying to watch the football game. She is upstairs sulking. You turn to your eight-year-old son and say, "Go upstairs. Tell that worthless mother of yours that I want the checkbook!" The child goes upstairs and soon returns. He reports, "Mom says over her dead body."

You turn to your son, "Go tell her, I want it right now or she'll have a shiner she won't forget for a month!" Five minutes later he returns, "Mom says, 'If you think you're man enough, go ahead.'"

Then, you tell him . . . . Wait. Stop right there. How do you think this kid is feeling?

Exercise 1.10 How the Child Is Feeling

_____
_____
_____
_____
_____

Using children to control or intimidate a partner may cause long-range problems for the child. Having a child relay messages such as the example above only confuses the child and can teach power and control tactics that later may be used on his or her own spouse. The child may come to believe that all relationships are like this. It also puts the child in a position of deciding who the "good guy" is and who the "bad guy" is.

In addition, some men use children to control their partner by making her feel guilty about them. "You are a terrible mother. How can you work all day and take care of the kids, too?" On the other hand, a man may threaten to take the children away. "If you do not do what I say, I'm going to call social services and have them take the kids." With such a threat, she is probably going to do what you want in the short term because her concern about the kids is very real.

Children also may be used during visitation. You are separated from your wife, but you pick the kids up for visitation. While doing so, you remind your wife of what a terrible mother she has been. You accuse her of being unfaithful, telling her she's fat or ugly. Whether the children are standing there is beside the point. You are engaging in power and control tactics through the use of your children. Again, you are setting an example for them. They are learning what relationships are like through your behavior.

Exercise 1.11 Using the Children

1. Have you used your children to try to intimidate or control a partner? Describe that action.

_____

_____

_____

_____

_____

Remember! Some people do not take partners in relationships—they take hostages!

Equality

What does equality in relationships mean? Basically, you might think of it as the opposite of power and control. In equal relationships, one person does not dictate actions and choices to the other. The dictionary defines *equal* "as great as; the same as" and "like or alike in quantity, degree, value" (*Random House Webster's College Dictionary*, 2001).

Some people bristle at the word "equality." They immediately think of "equal rights" movements and get the idea that their partner may try to control them. Some men who have been raised in a traditional culture may balk at the idea, thinking that they are the "king of the castle" and have the right to lord it over another person.

However, equality refers to **both** partners being treated equally. In fact, it might be thought of as "good news," whereby each partner treats the other with respect and honor. It is the basis of a positive and healthy relationship. What are the differences in behaviors between equal and power and control relationships?

Equality	Power and Control
Good communication	Poor or no communication
No threats	Coercion and threats
Compromise	No compromise; man decides all
Shared financial information	Man has control of all money
Shared decision-making	Man makes all decisions
Accountability	No accountability
Honesty	Honesty when it suits man's purpose
Shared responsibilities	Gender abuse
Safe, comfortable interactions	Intimidation
Trust, support, and respect	Isolation
Positive discussion	Jealousy
Responsible parenting	Using children in negative manner
Positive role modeling	Using children in negative manner

This list shows that treating your partner with equality includes healthy communication. Do you have good communication skills? Have you ever learned them? Or, when you have a different opinion from her, do you yell, holler, threaten, and try to get your own way? Do you understand the meaning of compromise? Unfortunately, people often are not taught relationship or communication skills in school—and, often, not at home. Later in this workbook, you will find sections on Communication and Problem-Solving. If you would like to review some of this early at your own pace, please do so.

Sharing financial information is critical in a relationship. A wise business owner would not hoard all of the information about his business. What if he should die? What if he suddenly were disabled? In a healthy relationship, sharing financial information is wise. Does the other person have access to the checking account or to funds to cover personal needs? Is the other person allowed to be a part of decisions made in the family?

Do you find excuses for your bad behaviors? For example, you blame the other person when you have an argument, but fail to see how you acted out. When you have a problem, you go to the bar and drink your troubles away, stating that you have a right to spend the money, since you earn it.

Taking responsibility for your actions is a very important part of equality. This means not blaming her, the system, or anyone else. Of course, situations affect your thinking and behavior. Words are powerful, and they affect us, but it is how you react to these situations and words that determine the outcome. Taking responsibility for your actions is the first (and a huge) step in making changes in your life.

Instead of intimidation, are you able to talk with the other person in a loving manner? Does the other person feel safe and comfortable talking with you when you have a different opinion or when there has been a conflict between you? Or, does she cringe and wait for you to wound her with your angry words—or actions?

Examine the role of trust, support, and respect in healthy relationships. Think about it. If you truly trust someone, why would you try to isolate that person from others? What are you afraid of? Will she meet someone else who is better-looking, richer, or smarter than you are? This, of course, also is part of the next item—jealousy. Some people do isolate others because they feel that the other person will leave them. Or, they may feel that the other person will discover that not everyone gets treated in a disrespectful, belittling manner. If they learn how other people live, they may try to leave.

Much of this boils down to positive discussion. Trying to use good communication skills, being honest with the other person, and making a good effort to avoid power and control tactics are keys to stronger relationships.

Another important concept in equality is being a responsible parent. That includes the avoidance of screaming, yelling, and putting each other down in front of the children. This does not mean that you never have a disagreement in front of the children, but that you handle such disagreements in a positive manner. You do not accuse her of sleeping around or threaten her in front of the children. You show your children by your actions how people act in healthy relationships. You do not use them to relay ugly messages to your partner.

Exercise 1.12 Power and Control

Part A.

1. Think of an incident in the past where you used any of the power and control tactics with a partner. Select another person in the group. Repeat the same language you used in one of these situations to that person. Try to use the same voice tone and expressions. Have the other person repeat your message back to you in the same way.

2. Now, discuss between the two of you how you think that felt to your partner.

3. Then, have the other person do the same thing with his incident.

4. Return to the group and talk about your reactions and how this relates to equality.

_____

_____

_____

_____

Part B.

Answer the following True or False. Then, we will discuss your answers as a group.

____ 1. How I act in front of my child may teach him that abuse is normal.

____ 2. All people fight (engage in physical abuse) in relationships.

____ 3. It is okay to call your partner a tramp when you are angry, if you do not mean it.

____ 4. Most jealousy is unfounded.

____ 5. Jealousy is often the result of insecurity and fear.

____ 6. Sharing financial information with your partner is foolish; she might try to spend all your money.

____ 7. It is okay to lie to your partner if you know she will get mad if you tell her the whole truth.

____ 8. Some work is women's work; some men's; that's just the way it is.

____ 9. Admitting that I have been violent in the past is a positive step forward.

____ 10. I may not like my partner's friends, but she has a right to them.

____ 11. Some opinions are just stupid, and I refuse to listen to them from my wife.

____ 12. Sometimes I might learn something from listening to my wife's opinions.

____ 13. A real man should not have to change a diaper.

____ 14. I make the money; therefore, she has no right to an opinion about how it is spent.

____ 15. She knew who I was when I married her; therefore, I refuse to change.

Definitions of Domestic Violence

Part C.

List at least five ways that you could improve the equality in your relationship—past or present.

1. _____
2. _____
3. _____
4. _____
5. _____

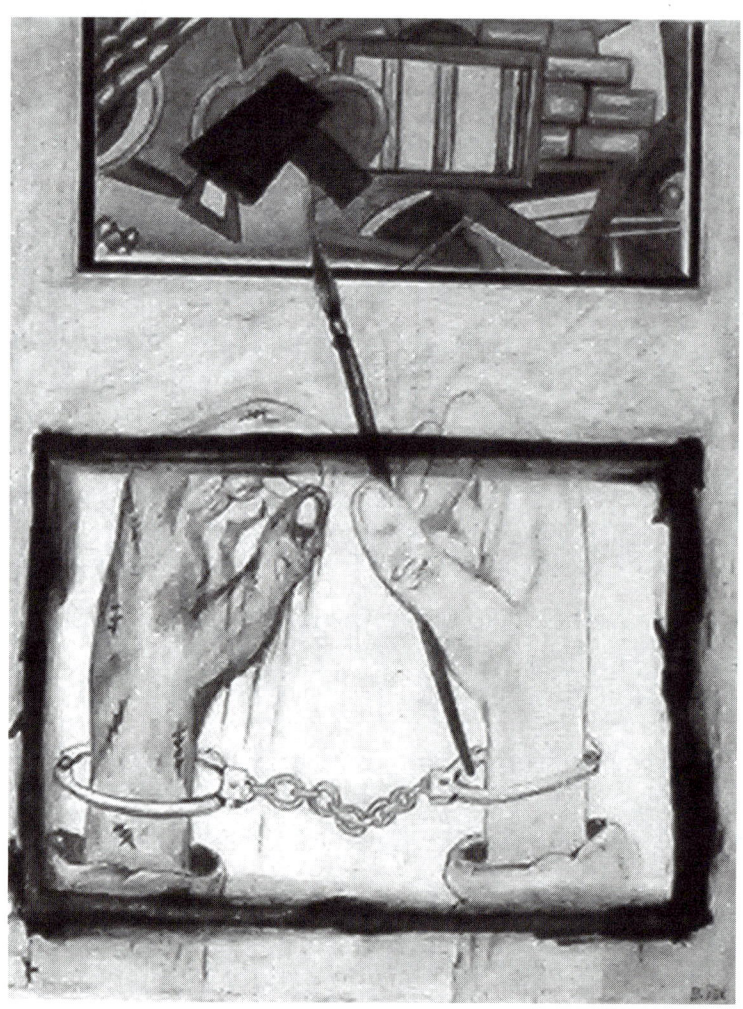

"Self-Portrait," by BP. Media: Pen and colored pencils on paper. Courtesy of Art Behind Bars.

Chapter 2: Basic Domestic Violence Issues
(3–5 Sessions)

Objectives

▶ To examine the impact of domestic violence through current facts

▶ To understand sources of domestic violence

▶ To explore various models that contribute to the development of domestic violence in cultures, societies, and the individual

▶ To examine personal characteristics that may have contributed to domestic violence behavior

▶ To continue working on personal responsibility

Domestic Violence Facts

You may be thinking, everyone argues—the law has overreacted to domestic violence. Or, you may think that what happens between two partners is their own business and everyone else should keep his or her nose out of it. However, current numbers show how prevalent domestic violence is in our society and with such prevalence it becomes a problem for society not just the individuals.

1. Estimates range from 960,000 incidents of violence against a current or former spouse, boyfriend, or girlfriend per year to 3 million women who are physically abused by a husband or boyfriend per year in the United States.

2. Nearly 25 percent of American women report being raped and/or physically assaulted by a current or former spouse, cohabiting partner, or date at some time in their lifetime, according to the National Violence Against Women Survey, conducted from November 1995 to May 1996.

3. As many as 324,000 women each year experience intimate partner violence during their pregnancy.

4. On average, more than three women are murdered by their husbands or boyfriends in this country every day. In 2000, 1,247 women were killed by an intimate partner. The same year, 440 men were killed by an intimate partner.

5. The health-related costs of rape, physical assault, stalking, and homicide, committed by intimate partners exceed $5.8 billion annually. Of that amount, nearly $4.1 billion is for direct medical and mental health care services, and nearly $1.7 billion is for the indirect costs of lost productivity or wages.

6. Approximately one in five female high school students reports being physically and/or sexually abused by a dating partner.

7. Studies suggest that between 3.3 to 10 million children witness some form of domestic violence annually.

8. In 2001, 41,740 women were victims of rape/sexual assault committed by an intimate partner.

9. Annually in the United States, 503,485 women are stalked by an intimate partner.

10. Intimate-partner violence is connected to various immediate and long-term health problems, which include physical injury, gastrointestinal disorders, chronic pain syndromes, depression, and suicidal behavior.

11. Fifty-three percent of victims of domestic violence were abused by a current or former boyfriend or girlfriend.

    (Sources are listed at the end of this unit.)

Exercise 2.1 Facts

1. Based on these facts, do you consider domestic violence to be

   ____ important but not critical?

   ____ somewhat important, but does not affect most people?

   ____ very important and far-reaching?

   ____ not important at all?

2. Review the facts again. Which facts can you associate with your situation?

_____

_____

_____

_____

_____

Myths Surrounding Domestic Violence

Numerous myths exist about domestic violence. You probably have heard some of these, or you may have repeated some of them to your friends or family. Examine them with an open mind and determine if you believe they are really true.

Myth #1: Some women like to be hit.

Do you like to be hit? Of course not. No one likes to be assaulted, except people who have psychological problems. Normal human beings do not like other people abusing them. Some women with low self-esteem may reason that they deserve to be abused or mistreated or that they have done something to deserve it. However, no one likes to be hit or abused in any way. Rather, victims of domestic violence desperately want the abuse to end and engage in various survival strategies (Dutton, 1994).

Myth #2: Once a batterer, always a batterer. They cannot control their violence.

Although some men may continue to batter, it is not because they have no control. Rather, they batter because they choose not to learn new skills, including anger management. Or, they batter because they choose to continue in the same patterns in their life, doing the same activities, reacting in the same way to situations that occur. People can change. They do change—but only if they want to and make the effort. Remember, change takes work.

Why is it that rarely does a man assault his wife in the grocery store or on the street? It is almost always in the privacy of his home. This means that he can control his behavior and can "pick and choose" when he will abuse her.

Myth #3: Battered people always can leave.

You may be saying to yourself, "If someone were beating on me, I'd just leave." That is easy to say. However, you may not be in the same position as a woman with two small children and few, if any, skills. Women stay in battering relationships for many reasons. Think about it. Here are just a few of the reasons:

- I have no job, no means of support. How can I take care of my children alone?
- My parents will be angry with me. They will say, "I told you so."
- What will the members of my church think? I took a vow: Till death do us part.
- I am afraid. He will come after me—hurt me—kill me—maybe even hurt the children.
- He will call the child protection team. They may take the kids away.

According to the Clark County Prosecutor's Office in Jefferson, Indiana, many factors keep the victim from leaving: housing, support, cultural or religious restraints. In addition, it has been estimated that the danger to a victim increases by 70 percent when she attempts to leave, as the abuser may escalate his use of violence when he begins to lose control (2005).

Myth #4: A couple must stay together for the sake of the children.

Imagine that you and your partner are continually fighting, arguing, cussing at each other, and bickering over the bills, household chores, everything. How do you think the children feel about that? What are they learning about the roles of husbands and wives in relationships?

Staying together for the sake of the children is prolonging the damage to the children. You are placing them at greater risk than if they were in a loving single-parent home.

One study indicated that child abuse occurs in up to 70 percent of families that experience domestic violence (Peled, Jaffe, and Edleson, 1995). Another study noted that 40 to 60 percent of men who abuse women also abuse children (American Psychological Association, 1996). In addition, children who witness domestic violence are more likely to exhibit behavioral and physical health problems including depression, anxiety, and violence toward peers (National Clearinghouse on Child Abuse and Neglect Information, 2003).

Myth #5: Violence is caused by alcohol or drugs or stress (or some other factor).

Perhaps you have said, "I wouldn't have touched her if I hadn't been drinking." After all, there is a close connection between violent behavior and alcohol abuse. However, alcohol or any other drug, stress, or whatever other reason you might use for explaining your abusive behavior does not work. These are simply excuses for your bad behavior. You made the choice to drink or use. Therefore, you are still responsible for the outcome. If you are stressed, it is your responsibility to take inventory of that stress and do something about it. Everyone gets stressed at times. It is a part of life. However, how you handle the stress (either in a positive way or a negative way) is up to you.

Jillson and Scott (1996) point out that substance abuse may increase the frequency or severity of violent episodes in some cases, but it does not cause perpetrators to abuse partners and frequently is used as an excuse.

Myth # 6: It is the woman's fault—She provoked me.

This is a very common statement, but unfounded. We are provoked every day in some way—by partners, coworkers, children, friends, or parents. If we beat up someone every time we were provoked, that is all we would be doing! Whatever the other person did to you, you still made the decision about how to react. It was your choice to be violent. The report on domestic violence from the Office of the District Attorney in Sedgwick County, Kansas, indicates that victim provocation is no more common in domestic violence than in any other crime.

Myth #7: Only a few people are affected by domestic violence.

Wrong. Many people are affected—people from all walks of life, every level of society, every income range. In addition, teenagers can beat up their partners or verbally abuse them. Some teens are in domestic violence programs. Senior citizens or the elderly often are overlooked when discussing domestic violence. The truth is that they, too, commit acts of assault. The report from Sedgwick County notes that people from all walks of life are battered, not just those in poor, poorly educated, or minority families. Batterers come from all income levels, professions, religions, ethnicities, and races.

Myth #8: She deserved it.

Regardless of what the other person has done to you or others, no one deserves to be assaulted. The person may have provoked you. She might have spent money you did not have. Maybe she struck you first. Regardless, no one deserves to be abused. Besides, violence never solves conflict in relationships. Responsibility still rests on the perpetrator.

As the Sedgwick County report states, "While our society derives from a patriarchal legal system that afforded men the right to physically chastise their wives and children, we do not live under such a system now. Women and children are no longer considered the property of men."

Myth #9: She must be crazy.

Again, this is blaming the victim for causing the abuse. Studies show that women in violent relationships are no more mentally disturbed than any other women. Often their behaviors, which we see as "crazy," are simply tactics used to survive in a dangerous and difficult situation.

A report from the American Bar Association states that while people with mental disabilities are not immune to being abused by spouses or intimate partners, they are not mentally ill. However, some victims may suffer from psychological effects, such as post-traumatic stress disorder as a result of being abused (Dutton, 1994).

Myth #10: If we just ignore it, it will get better.

One party or the couple wants to pretend their relationship will get better without any help. This often happens when the perpetrator refuses treatment. However, the truth is that change rarely happens without intervention. Even with the best counseling, change usually is a slow and difficult process. As Lenore Walker points out in her book Abused Women and Survivor Therapy (1995), women who have been abused in any way may require specific treatment to make changes in their thinking and behavior. Men, too, will rarely make changes in their thinking and behavior without some intervention, whether that is an arrest, jail time, or counseling. Ignoring a problem does not make it go away.

Exercise 2.2 Myths

1. Review the myths on the previous pages. Which myths have you believed in the past or currently? Why did you believe them?

_____
_____
_____
_____
_____

2. Is there any myth that you no longer believe? Which one(s)? Why?

_____
_____
_____
_____
_____

Where Does Domestic Violence Come From?

A number of theories exist to explain where domestic violence comes from. Have you ever thought about why you have been violent in the past? Where did you learn this behavior: from your parents, from television or movies, from your friends, or just from your own stress? All of these factors may help explain how people develop ideas of violence—and then act on them. Yet, theories do not take away personal responsibility. However you may have learned your behavior, remember you are still responsible for your actions.

Six theories attempt to explain domestic violence. Remember, these are just theories. No one theory in itself can completely explain human behavior, because human behavior is very complex. However, these theories can help you to understand how your thinking led you to abusing others. Perhaps, if you realize where you got certain ideas, you can develop a way to stop thinking in this manner in the future.

These theories are as follows:

1. **Psychiatric:** This model states that the source of violence is within the personality of the abuser. It assumes that that person is violent as the result of mental or emotional illness, psychopathology, or drug or alcohol abuse. In other words, a person who acts in an abusive manner toward another person must have a mental health disorder or a severe personality problem that contributes to the behavior. The perpetrator may drink or use drugs perhaps to cope with his problems or feelings of inferiority. Those substances may affect his behavior and then contribute to his violent tendencies. Basically, the idea is that the person's state of mind and personality are the reason for his or her violent behavior.

2. **Ecological:** This model examines development within a family environment and the family's development within the community. It looks at stress, lack of community support, and personalities that do not match within relationships, noting that such factors lead to increased risk for violence. The ecological model looks at the environment or surroundings of a person. It states that the family a person grows up with, as well as his peers and neighbors, affect his thinking and attitude. For example, a person who grows up in a neighborhood surrounded by gang violence and a family system where the parents periodically punch each other in the face will develop distorted ideas about relationships. In addition, social conditions affect a person's behavior. The lack of jobs, for example, may create additional stress, which may contribute to aggressive outbursts and violence. Poor medical care or childcare options are other factors that could affect the behavior of the individual.

3. **Patriarchy:** This theory looks at violence from a historical perspective. It examines the way women traditionally have been placed in subordinate positions to men, leading to power and control tactics by males. This theory states that women have been held to be of lesser value than men, dominated by them, and unable to rise to positions in employment, for example, just because they are women. The word "patriarchy" itself means "a form of social organization in which the father is the head of the family" or "an institution or organization in which power is held by and transferred through males" (*Random House Webster's College Dictionary*, 2001).

To some extent, this theory may have led to people condoning or supporting family violence. For example, the idea that the man is the head of the household and should be the decision maker, with little or no input from his spouse, stems from this notion. In addition, the idea that when a man beats his wife, it is his business or family business, and no one (or criminal agency) should be involved—also stems from patriarchal thinking.

4. **Social learning:** This model is related to the ecological and the patriarchy model because it starts within social structures. Social learning states that people learn violence from society and their families. In other words, if you watch your parents constantly fighting while you are growing up, you learn that is the way families behave. When you become an adult, you may end up treating your wife in the same manner. This is known as role-modeling.

Groups with few resources, such as the poor, are seen to be at greater risk for family violence than those who have more resources. In addition, social learning/situational theory states that violence arises from stress due to low income, illness, and cultural norms, such as spare the rod and spoil the child. This notion refers to the idea that beating or punishing children with a stick or other instrument to teach them rules is okay.

5. **Reward System:** In our interactions with others, we constantly weigh rewards against costs. When people abuse family members, "because they can," this theory is applied. The thinking is something like this: If I smack my wife, she will do what I say, and I am then rewarded by getting my way. Chances are no one will know, and if someone does find out, I can deal with that. They should mind their own business anyway! In other words, the rewards of violence outweigh the penalties.

However, the results or social control can include being arrested, losing social status, and getting divorced. If a man considers these consequences, he may elect not to abuse his partner. However, if it seems like no one will know and no cops will be called, the abuser may decide that the violence is worth the risk. In other words, he is rewarded for his bad behavior and, in fact, may continue that behavior.

6. **Domination:** Social systems are often based on force or the threat of force. When a person feels he or she has no resources, then that person is most likely to resort to violence to maintain a dominant position. For example, a person who has a menial job, with low income and poor skills or opportunity, may use violence to maintain a more powerful position over his or her partner.

As you can see from this list, different theories are used to explain how people develop abusive behavior. More than one theory may apply to how a person develops. A person could develop ideas about power and control from the patriarchy model, but he also may have watched his parents fighting, so he could be affected by the social learning model. Can you see how several of the theories might overlap and apply to why a person acts in a violent manner?

"Nurture," by RA. Media: Colored pencil and pen on paper. Courtesy of Art Behind Bars.

Exercise 2.3 Sources of Your Own Abusive Behavior

Consider your own past abusive behavior. List two theories or models mentioned that contributed to your behavior. Give an example of each and then discuss with your group how you feel this affected you and your relationship with a partner.

Theory   **Example**

_____   _____

     _____

     _____

_____   _____

     _____

Characteristics of a Batterer

You are in this class because you have been labeled as a "batterer." You may not like that term. Yet, if you review the definitions of abuse, you will find that you fit in this role. Therefore, it is important to take a look at your own characteristics or the factors which have contributed to your use of abuse. You may have acquired these traits from your family history, experiences in life, survival needs, or a variety of circumstances. Nevertheless, they are present.

Remember, no one social class, ethnic group, or religion has a monopoly on domestic violence. Research shows that people from all walks of life, social status, and cultural groups commit acts of violence. You might say, "But the people with money never get caught." While it is true that sometimes such individuals can hire private lawyers and plea bargain, they still have committed domestic violence. If you think about it, you probably can recall several celebrities and/or "rich" people in your own community who have committed domestic violence—whether they have been prosecuted or not.

Here are some characteristics present in some individuals who have abusive traits. Not all individuals will have all of these traits. They are common, but not absolute.

Factors Contributing to Abusive Traits

1. **Family history of chaos or abuse:** Children who grow up in chaotic and abusive homes tend to copy that behavior. Since they have never had a healthy family model, they may believe that their family is normal. When they then begin their own family, they may follow this abusive pattern.

2. **Poor impulse control:** This is an inability to control behavior. When faced with stress, such individuals just react, usually very quickly. This means they are prone to "fly off the handle," to attack another person with little, if any, healthy communication.

3. **Stressors:** These individuals appear to have many stressors in their lives. However, they do not appear to have any tools for handling stress. They revert back to the behaviors they have always used in the past—often behaviors involving assault.

4. **Dependency:** Batterers also tend to be very dependent on others. This may seem strange, because they use power and control tactics much of the time. In fact, they are also very needy and feel incomplete without another person in their life.

5. **Gratification:** Batterers also tend to focus on getting their needs met immediately. If a partner or another person does not provide them with the item or service they desire, they tend to get very agitated.

6. **Ego needs:** This goes along with the gratification. Batterers focus on "I." They place their needs above that of others. The world revolves around them. They show little consideration for others.

7. **Low self-esteem:** This goes hand-in-hand with dependency. Although the batterer may try to control his partner, he actually suffers from low self-esteem. In other words, he does not feel very good about himself. He suffers from poor self-confidence, and even may feel that he is worthless.

8. **Jealousy:** This also goes along with low self-esteem. The person who feels good about himself and his relationship will not have unrealistic jealousy. Remember, jealousy is basically another word for fear—fear my partner will leave me for another or a fear that the children or her friends or work or school will take up more of her time. Poor me! I'll be left all alone.

9. **Dr. Jekyll and Mr. Hyde:** Typically, the batterer presents two different faces. First, he is "Mr. Nice Guy," at least to the world. However, at home and with his family, he may act like a tyrant. On the other hand, sometimes he may be very loving and nice at home, but change very quickly and become a monster.

10. **Traditionalist:** Many batterers believe in male supremacy and a stereotyped masculine role. They may believe that a wife's place is in the home, "barefoot and pregnant." A man is the head of the household and what he says goes.

Exercise 2.4 Traits That Have Contributed to Your Use of Abuse

1. Examine the traits and factors in the prior list. Now, list the ones that have contributed to your use of abuse in the past.

_____
_____
_____
_____
_____
_____

2. Are there any traits that you have changed? Describe those.

_____
_____
_____
_____
_____
_____

3. Which traits would you like to change in the future?

___

Sources for Facts in this Chapter

Bureau of Justice Statistics. 2001. *Special Report: Intimate Partner Violence and Age of Victim, 1993–1999*. Washington, D.C.: Bureau of Justice Statistics

Bureau of Justice Statistics. February 2003. *Crime Data Brief, Intimate Partner Violence, 1993–2001*. Washington, D.C.: Bureau of Justice Statistics.

Centers for Disease Control and Prevention. April 2003. *Costs of Intimate Partner Violence against Women in the United States*. Atlanta: Centers for Disease Control and Prevention.

Centers for Disease Control and Prevention and the National Institute of Justice. July 2000. *Extent, Nature, and Consequences of Intimate Partner Violence*. Washington, D.C.: National Institute of Justice.

Commonwealth Fund. May 1999. *Health Concerns across a Woman's Lifespan: 1998 Survey of Women's Health*. New York: The Commonwealth Fund.

Gazmararian, J. A., R. Petersen, A. M. Spitz, M. M. Goodwin, L. E. Saltzman, and J. S. Marks. 2000. Violence and Reproductive Health: Current Knowledge and Future Research Directions. *Maternal and Child Health Journal*. 4(2): 79-84.

Schechter, S. and J. Edleson. 2000. *Domestic Violence and Children: Creating a Public Response*. New York: Center on Crime, Communities and Culture for the Open Society Institute.

Silverman, Jay G., Anita Raj, Lorelei A. Mucci, and Jeanne E. Hathaway. 2001. Dating Violence against Adolescent Girls and Associated Substance Use, Unhealthy Weight Control, Sexual Risk Behavior, Pregnancy, and Suicidality. *Journal of the American Medical Association*. Vol. 286, No. 5.

Tjaden, Patricia and Nancy Thoennes. 2000. *Extent, Nature, and Consequences of Intimate Partner Violence.* Washington, D.C.: National Institute of Justice.

U.S. Department of Justice. March 1998. *Violence by Intimates: Analysis of Data of Crimes by Current or Former Spouses, Boyfriends, and Girlfriends.* Washington, D.C.: U.S. Department of Justice.

World Health Organization. 2002. *Intimate Partner Violence.* http://www.who.int/violence injury prevention/violence/global campaign/en/ipvfacts.pdf.

"Broken Sword," by BP. Media: Zine collage on recycled cardboard sealed with coffee creamer. Courtesy of Art Behind Bars.

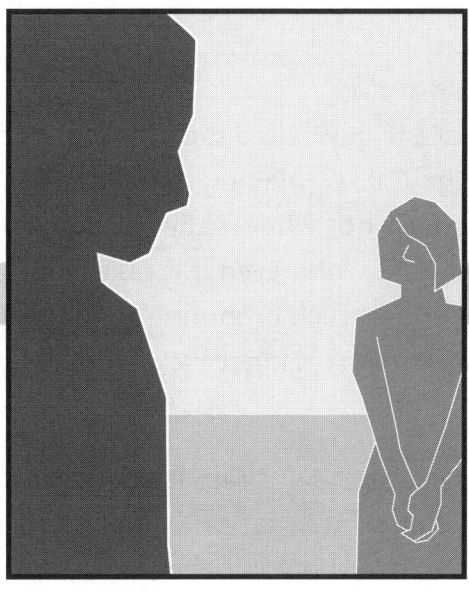

Chapter 3: Thinking Skills
(2–3 Sessions)

Objectives

▶ To understand the role of thinking and recognizing our thoughts in making choices

▶ To examine defenses used to justify actions

▶ To further develop accountability for choices and behaviors

The Perception/Recognition Model (ABC)

A	B		C
Action/Event +	Beliefs =	Choices with	Consequences/
	Perceptions/Awareness		Outcomes
	Values		

The above drawing shows how our actions result in certain behaviors or consequences. An action or event occurs (A). For example, someone calls you a dirty name. Your brain then processes this information, usually very swiftly, based on your awareness or beliefs about the situation (B). At that point, you make a decision (your choice) to react in a specific way (C)—strike him.

There is a tendency to think that the guy called me a dirty name, so, I just hit him. In other words, people tend to jump from A to C, placing the blame for the outcome on the other person or situation. However, this is not what really happens. B (your beliefs, perceptions/ awareness, and values) are always at work, even if it takes only a split second. For example, I am driving down the highway and a truck is coming at me in my lane. I do not need several minutes to make a decision. My survival instinct kicks in, and I pull over to the side of the road out of his way.

When someone calls you a dirty name, your brain is processing. Your reaction here is based on your beliefs or perceptions about the situation. What if this is a friend and he is joking around? What if it is your archenemy who you believe is out to get you? These are very different situations. You would have different reactions.

Much of how we act or react is based on our values or moral codes. If your code is that you do not do drugs, and you go into a house where people are doing drugs, then you probably will leave right away. If you know your moral code, it makes decision making much easier. Therefore, your values will play a large role in your choice—or the final outcome of the situation.

When you are faced with a decision, remember that you can **react** or **respond**. React means you just act without considering the consequences. You are angry. Therefore, you jump in. Respond, on the other hand, means that you stop and think about the situation and what is in your best interest and the best interest of those you love and care about, including society. That is where the choice part comes in.

Exercise 3.1 The ABC Model

Select one situation from your own experience and follow the model above. Describe how you responded or reacted and what the results were.

_____
_____
_____
_____
_____
_____

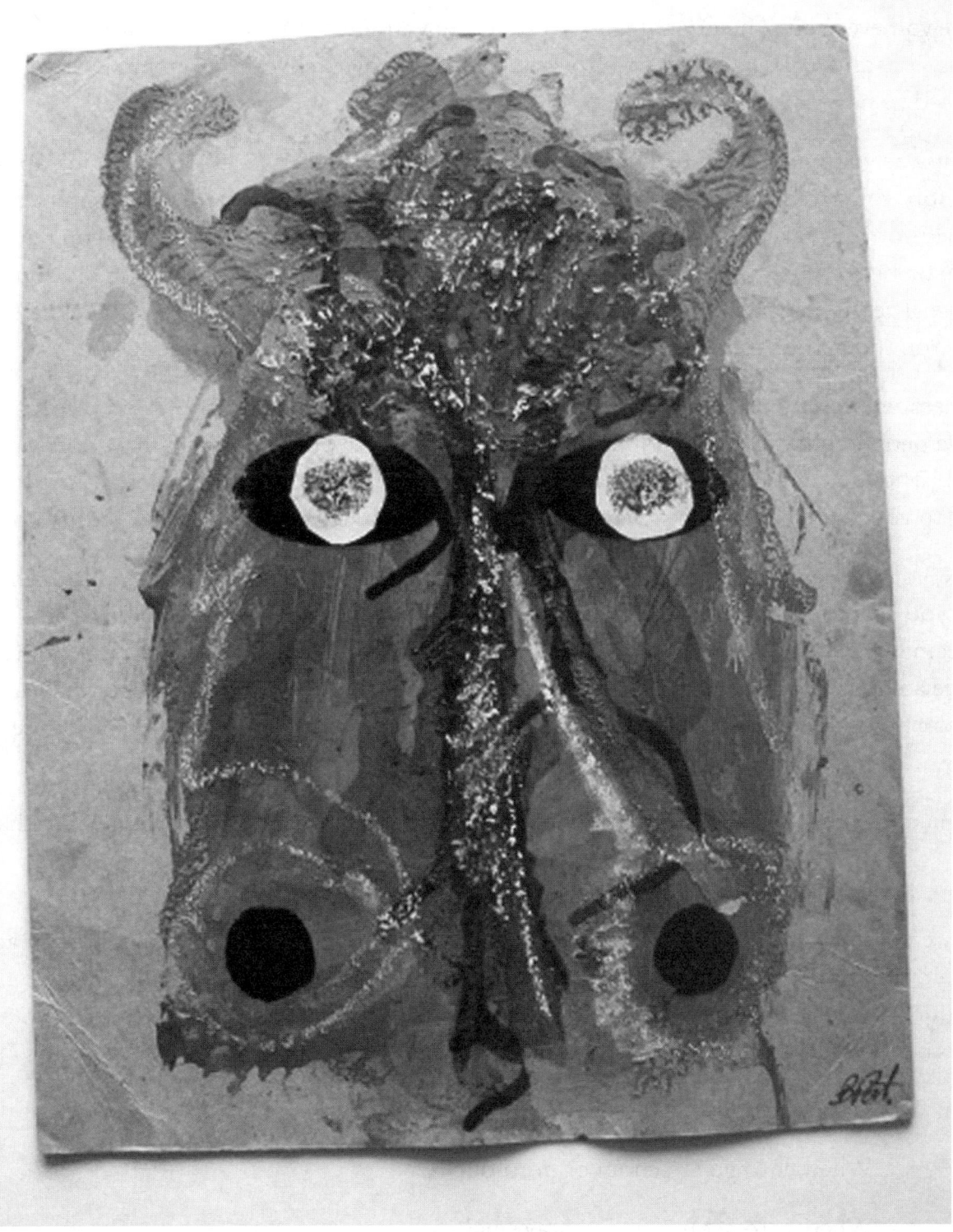

"Bull" by BP. Media: Kool-Aid™ powder, floor wax, homemade paint and marker on recycled cracker box. Courtesy of Art Behind Bars.

Choices

Have you ever had someone threaten to smash in your face? Or has someone ever called you a "bastard"? Or maybe the waitress spilled coffee all over your new pants? Or your wife refused to have sex with you?

What was your immediate reaction? Did you just "lose it"? Did you stop and think about it before you acted? Many people, when faced with a situation, immediately jump to a conclusion and take action. For example, someone calls you a dirty name. Do you believe that, therefore, they caused you to strike them? Many people believe that. You did something to me. Therefore, I had to hit you. You spilled coffee on me. Therefore, you made me cuss you out. You threatened me. Therefore, it is your fault that I smashed in your face.

Remember, **no one can make us do a thing. We always have a choice**. This is very hard for some people to understand. For example, you got up late one morning and were driving to work. The trucker in front of you was going the speed limit. You couldn't get around him. You said to yourself, "He's making me late." No, you are making yourself late by getting up late.

Now, you are probably thinking, "What do you mean, I always have a choice? No way." Yes, you do have a choice. Take a plea agreement, for example. You may not like the plea agreement, but you did not like the possible outcome of taking your case to trial. So, you made a choice. You may think it was not the best choice. But, it still was a choice. Even if a person holds a gun to your head, you still have a choice. You can comply or you can resist. Now, it may not be in your best interest to resist, but you still have that choice.

By making choices as you move through life, you create your own reality. Remember that:

You create your own reality!

How can this be true? Think about it. Every day you make choices—whether to get up at a certain time, whether to come to class, or go to work. All of these choices affect the outcome of your day, possibly tomorrow. If you are taking classes, that may help sway the parole board in your favor. Even if that does not happen, you may learn something useful in a class.

Think about your past choices:

- Whether to go to school or drop out
- Whether to get married or stay single
- Whether to rob the convenience store
- Whether to stop at the bar for a drink

- Whether to have unprotected sex
- Whether to buy a car you could not afford

Think about what effect these or other choices have had on your life.

Exercise 3.2 Past Choices

Look back on the choices you have made. Now, examine how these choices have led you to create your own reality. Describe the choices and what you might have done differently.

_____
_____
_____
_____
_____
_____

Your Defense System

Thinking Errors

All people have some thinking errors. Often, they do not even realize that they are errors until they are called to their attention. For example, have you ever thought, "I do not need any help. I can do it on my own"? This is a refusal to lean on other people, who might be supportive and helpful of your needs. Many thinking errors exist and the following are just a few. You may want to add some of your own to the list.

1. You can't trust anyone. Everyone is out to get you.
2. I have a right to take what I need from others.
3. My ideas are right; theirs are wrong.
4. I am superior to others (based on my race or religion).
5. All women are gold diggers.

6. They deserved exactly what they got.

7. The world owes me.

8. I did not hurt anyone by selling drugs; people make their own decisions to buy.

Exercise 3.3 Correcting Thinking Errors

Read each statement above carefully. Then, change the statement to correct the thinking error.

1. _____
2. _____
3. _____
4. _____
5. _____
6. _____
7. _____
8. _____

Role of Justifying, Minimizing, Denying, and Blaming

Although listed separately, these are also thinking errors, which we have previously discussed but they are so important that we need to go through these points again. These thinking errors often go beyond thinking and turn into behavior. For example, look at the following descriptions:

- **Justifying:** Trying to excuse one's actions or "make them right." It is a form of rationalization. For example, you get arrested for domestic violence and you tell people, "I do not normally behave like that. I was under so much stress. Who wouldn't fall apart?"

- **Minimizing:** This occurs when you try to make the situation less than it really was. You state, "It was just a verbal argument," when in fact you shoved or pushed your partner.

- **Denying:** This is when you flat out dispute that anything happened. "She lied. I never laid a hand on her," even though there might be physical evidence that an assault took place.

- **Blaming:** This occurs when you are putting your responsibility off on someone else. "She started it. She hit me first, and I was only defending myself."

Exercise 3.4 Correcting Other Thinking Errors

Select one thinking error that you have used most often. Discuss with your group how this has affected your relationship with any partner. If you are not working with a group, journal or write out this exercise and then review your answer.

"It Is Not Fair" Syndrome

Another defense mechanism occurs when a person falls into the "it is not fair" trap. This happens under a variety of circumstances. You are arrested and taken to jail. You may say, "It is not fair. She should have been arrested, too." And later: "It is not fair. She should have to do classes, too!" And then you go to treatment and say, "It is not fair. My neighbor, Bob, did domestic violence, and he got off without having to take any classes."

Well, **life is not always fair**. It is full of injustices. However, some of what you see as unfair is your failure to take responsibility for your own actions and to forgive the errors other people make as they move through life. Most of it boils down to your own defense mechanisms.

Exercise 3.5 It's Not Fair

For the next ten minutes, on your own paper, write down all the things you think are unfair in your life. This is your opportunity to vent. But you only have ten minutes. After that, you must stop. If you are working in a group, you may select a partner and you may take turns venting your feelings.

Whew! Now that you have that off your chest, take the next ten minutes and try to focus only on what things you think are fair. On your own paper, write down the things you think are fair. Be honest with yourself and remember the importance of taking responsibility for your own actions.

The Must and Should Trap

Some people get caught up in the "must and should" trap. It goes something like this: "My wife should have supper ready when I get home from work. She must obey my demands." Or "Everyone in the world must believe the same way I do about …" (fill in the blank (religion, race, ethics, values, and so forth).

Albert Ellis, the founder of Rational Emotive Behavior Therapy, has identified core irrational beliefs that lead to emotional problems. Among those are the three major musts (Clark, 2002). These include:

> **I must . . .**
> **You (he or she) must . . .**
> **The world and conditions under which I live must . . .**

People have a tendency to change their wishes to *musts*, *absolute shoulds*, and *demands*, which they then place on themselves and on others and the world. Then, they become unhappy and sometimes demanding when people do not comply with their wishes.

This can then lead to frustrations, even abusive situations. For example, if you think your wife SHOULD keep the house in perfect order or she MUST obey you when you make a demand and she does not, you may become agitated. Your expectations are not being met. Such regimented thinking only puts a wedge between you and your partner, and creates stress and anger within you.

Exercise 3.6 Musts and Shoulds

Recall a time when you used MUST or SHOULD demands with a partner. Describe what the result was. What could you have done differently?

_____

_____

_____

_____

Exercise 3.7 Thinking Errors

Read the following thinking errors and correct them.

A. It is okay to lie to your partner as long as she does not find out.

_____
_____
_____
_____

B. I am entitled to a few beers after work. After all, I work hard for my money.

_____
_____
_____
_____

C. You cannot trust women. All they want is a paycheck.

_____
_____
_____
_____

D. A man has a right to defend himself when a woman strikes him.

_____
_____
_____
_____

E. She knew who I was when we got married. I'm not about to change.

_____

_____

_____

_____

Accountability Concepts

What is Accountability?

To be accountable is to acknowledge and take responsibility for your actions. It means looking deeply at yourself and admitting to any abusive and violent behavior. It means recognizing that you cannot blame your behavior on others, or on stress, jealousy, alcohol or drugs, or childhood upbringing. Accountability means understanding that you must continue to work on yourself to prevent the destructive behavior from reoccurring.

How can I learn to take personal responsibility for my actions?

First, you need to acknowledge your abusive behavior. No change is possible until a person recognizes that there is a problem. Seeing your own abusive behavior for what it is, without blaming others, is a huge step. Following that, identify the acts you have done that are abusive. After this, identify the pain and losses that you have inflicted on your partner, children, and others. If possible, attempt to make amends to those you have hurt, unless that would cause them more pain and trouble. Finally, you need to acknowledge that your partner and others may be afraid of you and possibly never again trust you.

Remember, you cannot expect or deserve forgiveness from your partner or others you have injured. If they provide that forgiveness, it is wonderful, but do not expect it.

Provocation Is Not an Excuse

"I was provoked."

"A man can take only so much."

"She bitched at me night and day. Finally, I exploded."

People make these and other remarks in treatment. However, they are excuses for your bad behavior. People are provoked every day—at home, on the job, in the shopping center. If you lashed out and lost control every time someone provoked you, that is all you would be doing. The reality is that only YOU can control YOUR behavior. You cannot put the blame back on someone else.

Does this mean that other people do not contribute to our moods and feelings? Of course not. But learning healthy techniques for controlling your emotions and communicating your needs to others, including your partner, can go a long way in preventing domestic violence. In fact, it can go a long way in sustaining and promoting other healthy relationships, as well.

Exercise 3.8 Cost of My Behavior

Fill in the following blank as completely as you can:

The cost of my violent behavior (dollars, emotionally, in relationships) has been

_____
_____
_____
_____
_____
_____
_____

"Multifaceted Self-Portrait," by JS. Media: Crayon on recycled manila folder. Courtesy of Art Behind Bars.

Chapter 4: Communication
(3–4 Sessions)

Objectives

▶ To understand how language influences relationships

▶ To expand your knowledge of various types of communication, such as body language and listening

▶ To overcome barriers of communication

▶ To examine your communication and personality style

▶ To develop healthy communication

What Is Communication?

Communication is a word we throw around. When couples come for counseling, they are asked "What's the problem?" Usually, they will say "communication." What does that mean? Can they not talk to each other? Do they not listen? Do they speak different languages? Do they have different values or lifestyles? It is important to examine all the different parts of communication to better understand the role it plays in healthy relationships.

Communication is not just talking. It consists of several parts. As human beings, we communicate in a variety of ways. Along with talking, we should listen. We also use body language, touch, and sign language. We dance and listen to or make music. These are part of how we communicate.

We will examine some of these more closely.

Exercise 4.1 Communicating

Do you stop and really listen when someone is talking to you? Check off the activities that are typical of how you behave.

- ❑ Do you turn away from the television and give the person speaking your undivided attention?
- ❑ Or, do you interrupt her and not hear her out?
- ❑ Do you react swiftly without all the information?

If you checked the second or third box, try being quiet and listening. The person speaking will appreciate it. You may gain insight. Such insight may lead to a healthier relationship.

Body Language

Experts say that body language is 85 percent of communication. We can say one thing with our mouth and something else with our eyes, hands, shoulders, and expression.

Exercise 4.2 Body Language

You might ask your partner, "Is it okay if I go to the bar with the guys?" She might reply, "Sure, go ahead." But at the same time, her eyes were flashing, her nostrils flared, and she was making a fist. Not only that, but her tone was sarcastic. What is she really saying?

_____
_____
_____
_____

Gestures are another important part of sign language. Giving a person a "high sign" as opposed to "the finger" has very different meanings. Keep in mind that gestures can have different meanings to different people or different cultures or countries. For example, the "A-OK" sign often used by Americans can mean "A-hole" in some parts of the world. In other words, such a gesture can be very insulting.

- **Sign language:** This is a language developed for the hearing impaired. If you have ever seen anyone sign, you know how awesome that language is. However, we also sign without being hearing impaired, by our gestures and body language, the use of our hands (and fingers!), as noted above.

- **Writing (paper or electronic):** Another way to communicate is by writing. Whether you write a note, a letter, or a memo to a person, it is there—on paper for a person to react to—to ignore, to appreciate, or to hate. Many people communicate through e-mail, text messages, or in online chat rooms. Again, these are just forms of writing—and a person should be clear about what he is writing and its possible consequences.

- **Activities and Dress:** We let others know much about ourselves (or communicate with them) through our activities and our dress. For example, entering a person's home, you look around. What do you see? If they have CDs, do you scan the titles? What groups do they listen to? Do they have some DVDs on top of the TV? What are those titles? We judge people from what we see of their interests and how they dress. This is a part of communication. Take it a step further. What magazines do they read? *National Geographic*? *Sports Illustrated*?

Cultural interests such as music, art, dance, and dress all play a role in communication. In fact, these items can contribute to your becoming interested in another person—asking her out on a date. If you are into rap music and she is focused on country music, you may get the message that a relationship would never work.

- **Meaningful talk:** This is more than just making noise. Talk should be about real issues—at least at times. Of course, there is time for the trivial, fun talk—whether it is about the weather or a TV program. However, a healthy relationship includes meaningful conversation. You sit down, establish good eye contact, and actually discuss a mutual problem or just take time to let the other person know how important she is to you. Meaningful talk also can be done by telephone.

"Egg on My Face," by MM of Art After Bars. Media: very mixed on canvas. Courtesy of Art Behind Bars.

Exercise 4.3 Communication Improvement

Read through the types of communication listed previously. List the ways that you could improve your communication with your partner (now or in the past).

_____
_____
_____
_____
_____

Barriers to Communication

We communicate in many ways. Yet, many things can get in the way of understanding what someone is telling us. Did you ever misunderstand something someone said to you? Did your girlfriend ever tell you to meet her at a certain time or place and you could not remember the whole message—or you thought she said one thing when it was really something else? Did you ever hear a song and discover later that you misunderstood the lyrics?

Exercise 4.4 Barriers to Communication

We are all guilty of misunderstanding and miscommunicating at times. List some of the things that have gotten in the way of your communication.

_____
_____
_____
_____

Review these with your group.

Now, we will back up and discuss these and other barriers. Some barriers to communication include:

- **Listening:** If your mind is somewhere else, you are not listening. Then, it is going to be difficult to understand what someone is saying to you.

- **Speech:** If the other person mumbles or if she has a foreign accent that your ear is not used to, that will make hearing the correct message more difficult. If she speaks another language, of course, that will be a major stumbling block. If you are hard of hearing, mumble, or have a foreign accent, then the person listening to you will have added trouble. And, you will need to try harder to communicate more effectively. Sometimes, you may need to repeat things in different words or in a clearer manner. When you do, control your anger. It may not be the other person's fault that she did not hear you correctly.

- **Environment:** What if you are trying to talk in a crowd of other people? What if the TV or radio is on loudly when you are trying to talk or listen? What if other people—including her children—are talking to your partner at the same time?

- **Mental state:** What if you are depressed or feeling sad? What if you just received word that your parole was turned down? If so, your mind may not be on the conversation taking place beside you.

- **Anger:** This is also a mental state. When you are angry, you cannot think straight. You may make irrational decisions (see Chapter 7). You probably only half-hear what people say to you. You may misinterpret what they do or say, or fly off the handle at the slightest thing. The best thing you can do is to wait until your anger has passed before making decisions. It is also best to wait to talk about anything important until your anger has passed.

- **Physical health:** Have you ever had a splitting headache when you just did not want to talk with anyone? Have you ever had the flu or any other sickness when the last thing on your mind was "healthy communication?" This is another barrier to good communication. Perhaps your partner was not feeling well when you wanted to talk and she did not grasp what you were saying or reply in a way that made sense to you.

- **Other events/actions:** Life itself can get in the way of good communication. Any event or situation that affects you emotionally can create this barrier. What if a partner wants to talk just after you have been fired, or after receiving bad news about your mother's health? What if you want to talk but she has experienced these issues? People's actions and our perceptions or views of those actions can create problems in understanding.

With these barriers (and possibly more that you can think of), the wonder is that we communicate as effectively as we do! If you recognize that there are barriers, you can make a special effort to work around them. If the physical setting creates a temporary barrier, perhaps you can move to a different part of the room or another room. If your health is affecting the way you communicate, perhaps you can wait for another day to have any important conversations.

The Effect of Personality Styles

Think about the times when you have been trying to communicate with someone, and you could not seem to get through. Maybe it seemed like the two of you were speaking different languages. Maybe it seemed like the other person was not listening or did not care. But, consider this: perhaps the two of you have different personality styles. When communicating with other people, we often do not think about their personality style or adjust the way we talk to them. You might think by adjusting how you talk to them, you would be giving in. This is not true. It simply is using communication tools to assist you in getting your needs met. It also helps the other person to understand where you are coming from. Sometimes by making this adjustment, you can break down the communication barriers and develop better relationships with people, including your partner.

Let us look at some basic communication styles.

- **Passive:** Shy, quiet, soft-spoken, easily victimized, afraid to say "no," afraid of offending others for fear that they will not like you.

- **Aggressive:** Loud, boisterous, demanding, can get physical and hit the other person. Bossy, makes demands and does not consider the rights of others.

- **Passive-Aggressive:** Acts passive, nonassertive, but then gets angry, can be sneaky and seek revenge in subtle ways.

- **Assertive:** Speaks in a normal, but firm tone, considers the needs of others and does not violate those needs; asks, does not demand.

Exercise 4.5 Effects of Personality

Imagine yourself in the following situation:

You get a new cellmate who has to have a lower bunk because he has a back injury. You have had the lower bunk all along and like it. How will he act and how should you react to get the best result if he is the following way:

Passive:

Cellmate:

_____
_____
_____
_____

Your Reaction:

_____
_____
_____
_____

Aggressive:

Cellmate:

_____
_____
_____
_____

Your Reaction:

_____
_____
_____
_____

Passive-Aggressive:

Cellmate:
___
___
___
___

Your Reaction:
___
___
___
___

Assertive:

Cellmate:
___
___
___
___

Your Reaction:
___
___
___
___

2. **Which personality style is easiest to deal with?** ___

3. What does this mean to you?

___

Improving Communication

All of us can improve our communication. To do so, we need tools. You would not build a house without a hammer, a saw, and some nails! Similarly, how can you improve your communication without good tools? Read through the following suggestions to assist you with improving communication. Then, do the exercises.

Listening (Attentiveness): Be a good listener. You cannot get correct information if your mind is somewhere else. Sometimes you may have to force yourself to pay attention. When your mind starts to wander from a conversation, pull it back. Make yourself listen. Ask questions of the other person if you do not understand something. Repeat something they say to you. That helps you to remember.

Exercise 4.6 Listening

1. Have you ever been embarrassed when you were talking to someone and were not attentive, and then she asked you a question? What was the result?

___

Use of "I" Language: Have you ever been in a disagreement with your partner and she said something like, "I do not know what's the matter with you! You always keep blaming me! If you would just keep a decent job! If you would just help me around the house! If you would just be a better father!" Well, you get the idea.

The focus is on "**YOU**." Your partner just put you on the defensive by using "you" language. If you are like most people, you probably are going to react by attacking the other person. Now, you say something like, "Me, what do you mean me? How about you? You are not such a great mom yourself! And why do you never have dinner ready on time?" Now, the fight is on.

The idea here is to take the other person off the defensive. If you express your feelings about a situation without attacking the other person, you are more likely to get a positive result. For example, instead of the above language, try using "I" language.

For example, your partner stays out until 2 a.m. with her friends. You are very worried, angry, and upset. When she comes home, it is easy to react and say something like, "What's the matter with you? Don't you know what time it is? Where did you leave your head?" Again, this will put her on the defensive.

Instead, you can take a different tactic. "I was very worried when I didn't hear from you. Next time you're going to be late, please call me. I'd really appreciate it—I promise I'll do the same for you."

Or "I get very angry when people call me names like that. I'd appreciate it if you wouldn't do that in the future. Remember, I am not going to fight dirty."

When you use this kind of language, you are expressing your feelings without tearing the other person down. Instead, you are asking to get a need met, and you are sometimes making a promise—or giving the other person a benefit, too. While this language may not always work—there is no guarantee—it does allow you to get your feelings out. You should come away feeling much better about your progress and behavior.

Exercise 4.7 "You" Language

1. Relate an incident in which you used "You" language. What was the result?

_____

_____

_____

_____

2. How could you have used "I" language in this same incident? What do you expect would have happened?

_____
_____
_____
_____
_____

Requesting, Not Ordering: This concept is very important in dealing with others. It is critical in working with family members. Always ask first. Avoid ordering people around. No one likes to be treated like a servant. Refer to the next unit on relationships, where you will be encouraged not to treat your wife or partner like a servant. A simple "Could you please?" said in a nonsarcastic manner can go a long way. Most people will respond much better than if you simply demand that they do something.

Exercise 4.8 Requesting, Not Ordering

1. What is the difference between a request and an order? What is the key factor?

_____
_____
_____
_____
_____

2. Give an example of an order you have used on your partner. Next, rewrite it as a request.

_____
_____
_____
_____
_____

Role of Respect and Praise: This idea goes along with Request/Not Order. If you respect someone, you are less likely to make demands of them. Respect means you honor the other person. You trust her and consider her important in your life. When you respect people, you care about them. When you love them, it is important that you let them know. Praise their efforts. Our partners—and our children—are more likely to want to work with us, when we show this respect for them, and praise them—when appropriate. Then, they can support us emotionally.

Be careful with criticism. Yes, wise people do grow and learn from criticism. But, the trouble with criticism is that often it is not constructive. Usually, it is destructive and hurtful. So, keep your criticism to a minimum. When you do criticize, be certain that it is done with "I" language. Stress how much you care about the other person's well being.

Exercise 4.9 Respecting and Praising, Not Criticising

1. Recall a time when you failed to praise your partner. Maybe you used harsh criticism. What was the result on your relationship?

_____
_____
_____
_____

2. What would you like your partner to praise you for? Have you let her know?

_____
_____
_____
_____

Clarification: There is nothing wrong in asking for more information. Have you ever taken a new job where special terms were used? Someone asked you to please move the "thingamabob" from the "whatyoumaycallit." You went, "What......?" But, maybe you did not want to ask. Maybe you thought they would think you were stupid. So, you just muddled through. There is nothing wrong in asking for clarification. It is important in family relationships. If you do not "get it," ask. In fact, people are often flattered when you ask them to explain a situation or ask them for more information. If you are embarrassed by asking, think about how you can say it. Maybe something like, "That's very interesting. Could you tell me more?" Or "I never heard that word before. Guess I'm out of it. Can you help me understand?" Some people will go, "All right!" It makes them feel smart.

Exercise 4.10 Clarification

Write about a situation in your relationship or currently that could have been better if you had asked for clarification.

_____

_____

_____

_____

_____

Repeat Information: Sometimes we need help to lock information into our brains. For example, pretend you are heading out the door to work and your wife mumbles something like, "Bring a quart of milk and loaf of bread on your way home tonight." You are in a hurry to get to work. You mutter, "Uh-huh" and away you go. Eight hours later, are you going to remember? Probably not.

One way to help overcome this problem is to repeat the information. That way, you know what you heard is accurate. Repeating information also stores it better in your brain. So, when your wife gives you the instructions, a good idea is to look at her and repeat, "Okay. I'll pick up a quart of milk and loaf of bread before I come home" or whatever it is she was stating. Of course, you can always write it down, but sometimes instructions and information come to us quickly and a pencil is not handy.

Exercise 4.11 Repeat Information

Group Work: Make up a request for another group member. Now, ask that person to do what you want. Each group member should repeat the request back. Do this exercise several times with different members of the group, so you can get into the habit of repeating back requests.

Biases: Our biases or prejudices can create many problems. For example, "All women are gold diggers. All they want is money." "He's a stupid liberal (or right wing pig!)." "All mother-in-laws are witches!" Biases and stereotypes can rob you of opportunities for healthy, interesting relationships. They can create roadblocks to your creativity and growth. Try to remain open-minded about people and situations until you have factual evidence pointing you in another direction.

Exercise 4.12 Bias

Can you think of other biases that could create problems in the relationship with your wife or girlfriend? List several.

_____
_____
_____
_____
_____

Magic Words: Words can be harmful. They can bring you down or lift you up. Have you ever gotten into an argument with someone when the argument got out of control? She was yelling at you, and you were yelling even louder. She called you a name. You called her a worse name. The situation continued to escalate until someone threw a plate or the police came. One of the ways to stop this kind of situation is to use "magic words."

What are magic words? They are words that stop the other person from topping you. They are words that are respectful. They happen when you are using assertive tools. Here are some examples of "magic words."

> **You might be right.**
> **I never thought of it that way.**
> **That's a good point.**
> **That's an interesting way to see it.**
> **I'd like to think about this tonight. Can we talk again in the morning?**

Imagine yourself arguing with your spouse. She is trying her hardest to convince you not to buy that car you looked at today. You really want to buy it. You think you can afford it. But you see the argument getting out of control. Instead of continuing the power struggle, you stop and calmly say to her, "You might be right."

This does not mean that you are giving in. You are acknowledging her point of view. Later, when you are both feeling calm, you can sit down and talk about the issue again. But for now, in the heat of the battle, you have stopped the argument.

Exercise 4.13 Magic Words

Group Work: Recall an argument in the past with a partner that got out of control. Discuss it with your group. What other language could you have used to stop the incident? Practice this out loud with your group.

_____
_____
_____
_____
_____

Who Owns the Problem? One of the key problems in communication is that we often try to take on the problems of other people. Whether it is our spouse, another family member, or a friend, we need to separate our problems from theirs. We need to focus on our own problems and quit giving advice or interfering with others. We also need to remember that people need to be responsible for their own actions. There is nothing wrong with listening and emotionally supporting people we love. But when we try to control the other person's actions, or try to "save" them, sometimes it can backfire on us. Instead, focus on your own problems, and avoid unwanted interference in the lives of others. You may find that you remove much confusion and chaos by focusing on your own problems.

Exercise 4.14 Ownership of Problems

Group Work: Recall a time when you tried to help with someone else's problem and it created more problems. Share this with your group.

_____
_____
_____
_____
_____

Staying in the "Here and Now": Picture yourself in an argument with your wife. She says, "I saw how you were looking at Mary last night!"

You reply, "Me? You're worried about me. Do not forget the way you were hanging on Sam at the company picnic in June!"

Do you see what is happening? The disagreement is moving from the concern about last night—or the now—into something that happened months ago. This happens frequently in arguments. People keep throwing up "old baggage" to each other. As a result, they argue in circles and nothing gets resolved. One of the key ways to resolve a problem is to stay on subject. Refuse to throw up the "old baggage." If you really have forgiven a past offense, then it should not be mentioned again.

Exercise 4.15 Old Baggage

Describe a past incident when you argued with your partner and you used the "Old Baggage" tactic to try to hurt the other person.

_____
_____
_____
_____
_____

Communication

Avoid Mind-Reading: Often, we think we know what the other person is saying. We do NOT. Even if you have been married to someone for ten years, you still cannot read her mind. Do not even try. And, do not ASSUME you know what she is thinking or feeling. You almost always will be wrong.

Exercise 4.16 Mind Reading

Have you ever had someone try to read your mind or put words in your mouth? Describe how that made you feel.

_____
_____
_____
_____
_____

Avoid the Silent Treatment: One of the tactics that makes a partner really angry occurs when the other partner refuses to talk about a situation. If your partner just shrugs her shoulders and walks away, it can be very infuriating. It can create another argument! Avoid this behavior. If you need time to think about an issue, tell your partner. "I need to think about this. Give me a few minutes alone." Do not just walk away. Your partner will get the idea that you do not care, that you do not want to work on the problem.

Exercise 4.17 The Silent Treatment

Are you a person who uses the silent treatment? If so, what has been the result? If you do not use this tactic, imagine what the result might be and describe that.

_____
_____
_____
_____
_____

Apologize: There is nothing wrong with an apology. It shows that you are man enough to admit when you are wrong. Sometimes it is okay to apologize when you are not wrong, when the other person has made the error. Business people do it all the time. "My mistake, sir," they'll say to a customer.

Exercise 4.18 Apologize

Do you have trouble admitting when you are wrong? How does it make you feel to apologize?

_____
_____
_____
_____
_____

Set Ground Rules: Healthy relationships have ground rules. If you do not have these in your relationship, you might consider working on them. Ground rules can focus on arguments. What do the two of you do when a disagreement occurs? Do you take a time out? Do you get sullen and refuse to talk? To communicate effectively with your partner, you both need to "be on the same page."

You need to have a good understanding of what is going to happen if an argument occurs. You also need ground rules in other areas of your relationship. Review the information in the relationship unit (coming up next) for more tips.

Remember—There Are Many Realities

Just because you see the world in a certain way, does not mean that your partner sees it the same way. Allow room for the realities of other people in your life. When you recognize that you and they are human and thus imperfect, you may find that your communication greatly improves!

"Man in a Small Window" by BP. Media: Mustard, homemade paint, coffee creamer, toothpaste, and baby powder on a brown paper bag. Courtesy of Art Behind Bars.

Exercise 4.19 Ground Rules

Group Work.

1. Did you and your partner ever have ground rules or did you make rules up as you went along? Describe to your group how this worked in your relationship.

_____
_____
_____
_____
_____

2. Make a list of three-to-five ground rules that you now would like to use in your relationship or in a new relationship.

_____
_____
_____
_____
_____

3. Why do you think these new ground rules could be helpful?

_____
_____
_____
_____
_____

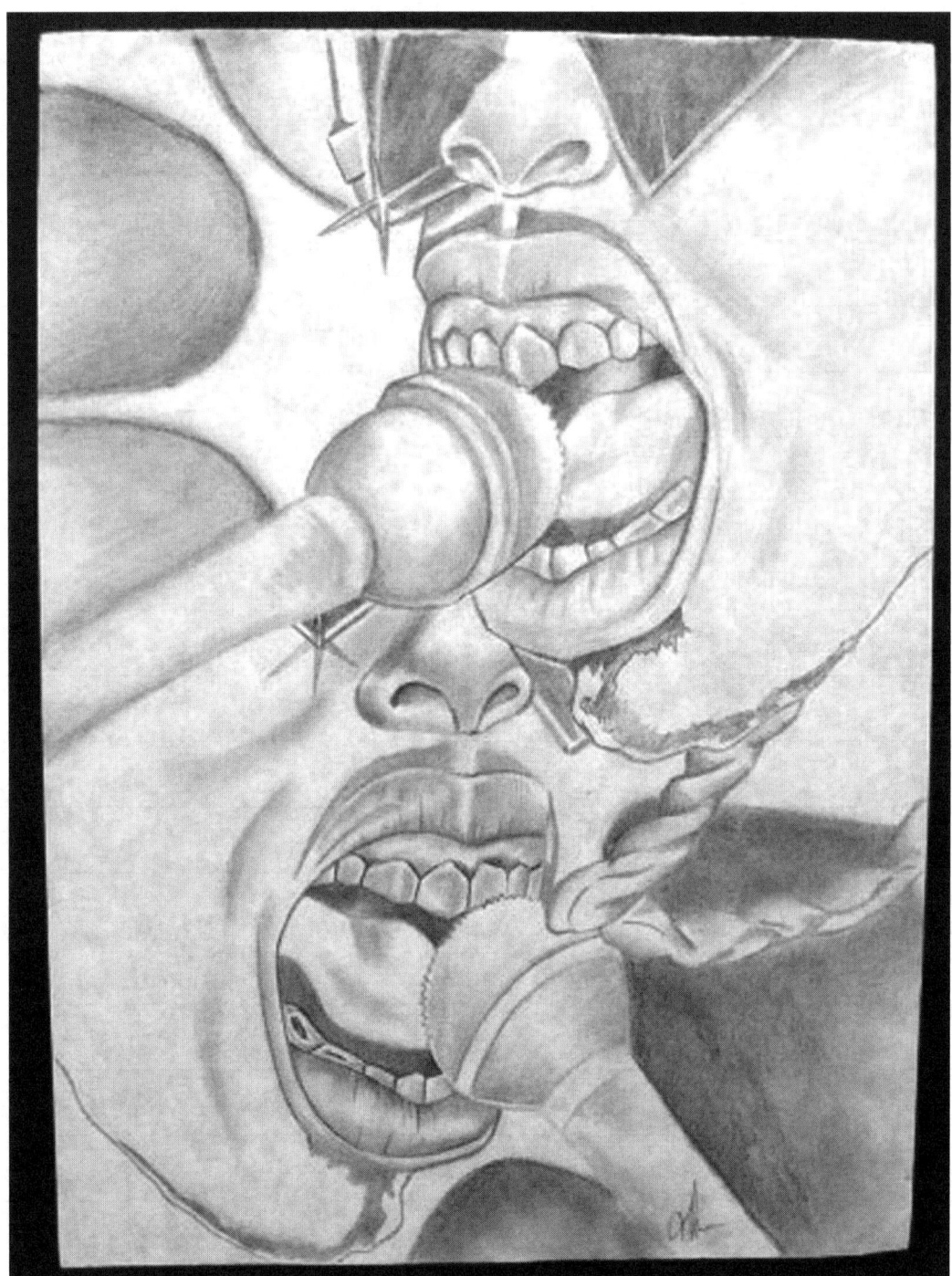

"Voices" by MT. Media: Pencil on paper. Courtesy of Art Behind Bars.

Chapter 5: Relationships
(3–5 Sessions)

Objectives

▶ To understand the impact of family systems on my development

▶ To avoid blaming families and systems for my actions

▶ To examine and understand negative factors in intimate relationships

▶ To develop victim empathy

▶ To understand the impact of domestic violence on children

▶ To acknowledge ways I have harmed my partner and children

▶ To build skills in developing healthy relationships

Effects of Relationships

What do you usually think about when you hear the words "domestic violence?" Is it two people fighting—husband and wife, girlfriend and boyfriend? Maybe you thought that domestic violence only affected you and your partner. Maybe you thought that it was no one's business but yours. If so, you are wrong. Many people can be affected by your actions. Some of those affected include:

- Spouse/Partner
- Children
- Parents
- Other Family Members
- Friends
- Acquaintances
- Employers
- Coworkers
- Community

Exercise 5.1 People Affected by Your Domestic Violence

1. You may think that some of the people mentioned are not affected by your domestic violence, but this is not true. Write one way in which each group might be affected.

Employers _____

Coworkers _____

The community _____

Acquaintances _____

2. Name the people above who were affected by your latest domestic violence incident—to what group from the above list do they belong?

_____
_____
_____
_____

Learned Behavior

Are you ever affected by how other people act? Think back to a time when you were a child. If you watched your parents scream and yell at each other, maybe you thought all relationships were like that. If you grew up watching dad strike mom when she "got out of hand," you may see that as normal. If mom "obeyed" dad when he got angry and struck her, you may believe that is the way to get your needs met.

As you got older, maybe you heard your friend brag about beating up his "old lady." Maybe you think that is normal, too, or even funny. Or maybe you have watched a video where a singer called a woman "a ho" and you accepted that as okay. It is no big deal, you thought. And maybe you have even copied some of these behaviors.

How did you learn what was "good" or "bad" behavior? You probably learned by watching your parents and caretakers. Later on, you probably learned more behaviors from peers, friends, and the world around you—yes, even television and film. This is called *learned behavior*.

Exercise 5.2 Learned Behavior

List your past or present actions or behavior that you may have learned from watching or hearing other people. These actions do not have to be related to domestic violence, if you did not witness this type of behavior growing up. You may use other examples as well.

_____

_____

_____

_____

Remember that not all people have to witness domestic violence to become a perpetrator. While witnessing violence may increase the risk, it is not absolute. Some people who rarely witnessed violence as children may grow up to be abusers. Others who witnessed violence may never abuse others. Many factors play a role as to how children respond. Those who have strong protective factors, such as social competence, high self-esteem, strong friends, and a supportive adult may never abuse others. Therefore, even with emotional or physical violence in the home, they may feel less of an impact than other children.

"Macho Man Showing Muscle" by BP. Media: Ink, baby powder, colored pencil, marker, and coffee creamer on recycled paper. Courtesy of Art Behind Bars.

Family Systems

What kind of family did you grow up in? Remember the words "learned behavior." Our family systems can greatly affect the way we see the world. If your dad came home drunk every Friday night, maybe you do that, too. You may find that you treat your partner the same way your father treated your mother. Does that sound impossible? Think about it the next time you lose your temper and threaten to "smash her face." We will look at three types of family systems and see why they can affect people so much.

RIGID	HEALTHY	CHAOTIC
Many rules	Rules, but flexible	No rules or rules
Strict enforcement	Good communication	Constant changes
Much criticism, sarcasm	Consequences logical, realistic	Inconsistent punishment
Threats, bribes used often		Many second chances
Surrounded by fear	Good support system	Emotions rule parents' decisions
Dictatorship atmosphere	Group decision making	
Conditional love	Unconditional love	Conditional love

As we look at these systems, think about the way your parents or caretakers acted toward you, your siblings, and each other.

The Rigid Family System. In this system, there are many rules, and the rules are never to be broken. When children break the rules, they are harshly punished. The punishment may be spanking or having weapons, such as boards, belts, or switches used on you. In this family, one person is usually "the boss" and demands that everyone else obey him. If he "cracks the whip," everyone else must jump. If you grew up in this family, you might have had a lot of fear. Maybe you were afraid of getting bad grades and being severely punished, or even punished for an innocent remark. Maybe you felt that you could never live up to the expectations of the "dictator" parent. Love in this system is conditional on a child obeying the rules.

The Chaotic Family System. In this system, rules are constantly changing, if there are rules at all. Much of what occurs depends on the feelings of the parent at the moment. If you lived in this family, your parents might let you get away with staying out past midnight on a school night—one time—but the next time, you were cruelly punished. Sometimes it is okay, sometimes not. This is sometimes known as the permissive family system. Can you see why this is confusing to a small child? Maybe when you got older, you got in trouble with the police, even got sent to jail, but your parents bailed you out—two, three, four times. In this family, parents tend to give children, second, third, and fourth chances when the children "mess up." But they give little in the way of consequences or positive guidance. Often, these families "live on the edge" and have substance abuse problems. Love is conditional on how the parent is feeling at that time.

The Healthy Family System. The healthy family system is what parents should aim for. In this system, there are rules. (We all need rules.) However, the rules are flexible. While consistency is important, on a special occasion a rule can be broken. For example, your bedtime was 8:00 p.m. and it was the Christmas holidays. *Frosty the Snowman* will be on at 8:00 p.m. That night you would be allowed to remain up for the show. If you grew up in this family, yes, you would get in "trouble" if you messed up. However, the discipline was logical, and consequences were realistic and consistent. Your family probably stood behind you when you made mistakes. You probably were allowed to express your opinion without the fear of being "put down" or made to look stupid. In this family, children are loved unconditionally. This does not mean the parents approved of bad behavior, but they were able to separate the bad behavior from the person.

Family systems can fall at different points on the scale. Some families are chaotic, but not extremely so. Some are rigid, but at times show more flexibility. In other words, there are degrees along the scale. In addition, sometimes one parent may be chaotic, while another is rigid. One parent might be healthy and the other chaotic. These mixtures can create special problems within the family, and they can be very confusing to children.

Exercise 5.3 Family Systems

1. Identify the family system involved. Write the correct letter in front of each behavior.

      A. Rigid   B. Healthy   C. Chaotic

____ 1. No rules or rules change all the time.

____ 2. Listen when their children talk.

____ 3. Lets their children stay up to whenever the kids want to go to bed.

____ 4. One person is the "boss" and calls all the shots.

____ 5. People who break rules are harshly punished.

____ 6. People who break rules are fairly disciplined.

____ 7. Give the children many chances, few consequences.

____ 8. This family is flexible.

2. Review the above family systems and think about the system in which you grew up.

    A. Which type most closely resembles that system?

    B. Do you see yourself using these same behaviors on your family now?

    C. Which behaviors do you use now?

    D. And which behaviors would you like to change?

_____
_____
_____
_____
_____
_____
_____
_____
_____

Personality Influences

Remember the words **learned behavior**. Yes, we are affected by the behavior we learned in our families while growing up. You were affected, but it is important to know that domestic violence behavior is not inherited. If you witnessed your father blowing up at the kitchen table, because the meat was too tough, you may believe this behavior is normal. Maybe your mother said something like, "It's okay. He has a short temper." Now you, too, say, "Sorry, but I have a short temper." No, you did not inherit your father's short temper. Such characteristics are learned.

Or, you watched your mother tremble and shake when your dad raised his fist. She backed into a corner. Now, you, too, back away from trouble. You do not walk away; you run. Maybe you allow other people to have their way because you learned that mom survived that way.

As you grow up, you may imitate the behavior you witnessed in your family. You may become a perpetrator or a victim. This does NOT mean you have to stay this way. We humans have super brains, more complex than any computer. Therefore, we can make positive changes in our lives, if we choose to do so. We can make conscious decisions to change. But change is not always easy, and learned behavior is a powerful chain, especially if it gets reinforced.

Reinforcement occurs when you receive more than one message that a certain behavior is a "good" thing. This can happen if you believe that the behavior got positive results. When dad hit mom, she obeyed him. Or perhaps he just threatened to leave her or to take the children away (emotional abuse). As a result, she did exactly what he requested. Perhaps you witnessed this type of behavior many times while growing up. Now, you see it again with your peers. When your friend bullies others, they give him their money. Guess what? It works. Now, you have seen several instances of this, and it reinforces your belief that this behavior works.

Remember, we are shaped by the ideas and feelings we develop early in life. These ideas and feelings form our personality and can affect how we handle conflict. For example, if you have a "short temper," what happens when you get into an argument with your girlfriend? Do you listen carefully and hear her side of the story? Do you explode? Do you accuse her of being unfaithful?

Some of the characteristics that people develop in unhealthy families and by their experiences can include:

- **Poor impulse control:** You lose your temper easily and do not consider consequences.

- **Dependency on others:** You rely on others to make decisions and are fearful of decisions.

- **Need for instant gratification:** You have to have your needs met immediately. You cannot wait.

- **Low self-esteem:** You have no self-confidence. You feel unworthy or even lousy about yourself.

- **Lack of trust:** People have to prove themselves. You are fearful that others are up to no good, or are out to get you, or take advantage of you.

- **Jealousy:** This goes along with a lack of trust and poor self-esteem. Fear drives jealousy.

- **Overdramatic responses:** You overreact to the smallest slight. Everything is a crisis.

What do all these traits have in common? Many of them are found in domestic violence offenders. Domestic violence offenders may not have all the characteristics, but most have low self-esteem, lack trust, are jealous, and have poor impulse control.

Exercise 5.4 Personality Characteristics

Read the list above.

A. What characteristics do you see in yourself?

B. List any you would like to change.

C. Describe why you would like to change them.

_____

_____

_____

_____

Avoiding Blame

After thinking about how families and other relationships may have affected your thinking, you may be tempted to blame your choices and behavior on them. Do not do so. You are responsible for your own choices. You are responsible if you are now in jail or prison. No matter what others may have done to you, you are now accountable for your own actions. It is too easy to blame others. It is too easy to make excuses. It is just another way to take the heat off you.

Some people have said, "I am in prison because I was raised in a bad neighborhood. My dad left when I was a baby. My mom was a crack addict." All of this may be true and regrettable. Nevertheless, many people have survived horrible conditions as children. Many of them have broken those chains and have become productive people. A shining example of this is author and counselor Dave Pelzer, who grew up in an extremely abusive home. His story is told in *A Boy Called It*. Pelzer went on to be recognized by several presidents for his outstanding work with youth. He overcame tremendous odds after being one of the most abused children in California. He easily could have ended up behind bars. He could have said, "My parents divorced. My mother starved me and beat me. I fell behind in school. I was in and out of foster care." But he did not.

It is also easy to blame the system. If you are in jail or prison, you may be saying, "The law isn't fair;" "The judge was out to get me;" "I couldn't afford a decent lawyer;" "I was set up" and so forth. But if you are truly honest with yourself, you did something. In fact, you probably did several things. Most people do not go to prison on the first misdemeanor. Think about it. Face it.

Many perpetrators use "provocation" as a way to cast blame on someone else and take the heat off of them. Perhaps you have made statements like, "She was calling me names, nitpicking. She said I was less than a man. A man can take only so much." You used this as an excuse for your abuse. Provocation is no excuse. People get provoked daily, in every walk of life, by bosses, family members, and by total strangers. But they do not turn around and assault them. Learning to control your anger is a key element. Do not blame your bad behavior on provocation.

Do not blame it on drugs and alcohol either. Many people drink or use other substances, but never attack other people. And some people who never use substances assault others. Yes, there is a connection between substance use and violence. But that connection has to do with the loss of judgment that occurs when under the influence. You made a choice to use the substance. Therefore, the blame goes right back to your doorstep.

Remember the old saying, "It is not the hand we are dealt in life, but how we play it." Take responsibility for your choices. Acknowledge mistakes. Learn from your mistakes. You cannot make positive changes in your life until you do this.

Exercise 5.5 Blaming Others

1. Who or what have you blamed in the past for your choices?

_____
_____
_____
_____
_____

2. Why do you think you were blaming someone or something else?

_____
_____
_____
_____
_____

3. In the future, what could you do differently to avoid blaming others?

_____
_____
_____
_____
_____

Intimate Relationships

So far, we have been talking about the influence of families and other experiences on your life. Now, we get more specific and examine the role of intimate relationships. First, what does intimate mean? Here it refers to relationships which include: spouses, common-law couples, cohabitating couples, dating couples, ex-spouses and ex-couples, as well as same-sex partners.

This list is divided into both common-law and cohabitating because some states recognize common-law marriage, but many states do not. Yet, many couples live together anyway or "cohabitate" without being officially married. And, very importantly, domestic violence laws in some states may pertain to all of these couples.

Intimate does NOT just refer to sexual relations, although it implies that. Intimate also means "sharing." Being intimate may include living in the same apartment, communicating well with each other, having a spiritual and emotional relationship, being committed to each other, and helping each other in good times and bad times. Does this sound like love? While you may not now be "in love" with an ex-partner, at one time you probably were convinced of your feelings.

Exercise 5.6 Intimate Relationships

List the type(s) of intimate relationships you have been in, in the past and currently.

_____
_____
_____
_____
_____

Now, we will examine some of the important factors in intimate relationships.

Positive Influences: Have you ever gotten fired from a job? Have you ever lost a $20 bill you needed for gas? Have you been accused of something you didn't do? If so, you know how it helps if you have someone to talk to—a wife, a girlfriend, a lover—someone who says, "I understand. I'll be there for you." This type of support may have kept you going, when all else fell apart. Perhaps it is even keeping you going now. Just knowing that someone is there for you when the world gets crazy can lift your spirit.

This is called *commitment*. It also is connected with stability. Sure, having a place to live, a job, and a little money is stability. But stability is also a relationship you can count on. Isn't it nice to know if you decided to go back to school, your friend would support your decision? Maybe she even would help you study. In life, we go through hills and valleys. The hills are wonderful—those days when it seems nothing can go wrong. But then, the valleys come. If you do not have a solid support system, if you do not have people who care, the road can be difficult.

Exercise 5.7 Positive Influences

1. Who cares for you? List the people who support you, who have been there through the "thick and thin."

_____
_____
_____
_____

Hands Down: A Domestic Violence Treatment Workbook

2. How does it make you feel to have this support system? If you do not have a support system at this time, describe how that makes you feel.

_____

_____

_____

_____

_____

False Expectations: One of the greatest problems faced in relationships is that of false expectations. For example, do you expect your wife to look like the July Playmate of the Month? If you do, and she does not, that can create friction. Do you expect her to cook like your mother did? What if she does not even like the kitchen? Do you expect that she will drop all of her friends because she now has you? That probably will not happen. Do you see where this is going? If you have certain "false expectations" around a relationship and your partner does not live up to them, you may find yourself arguing a lot.

Many things lead to problems in relationship—communication, sexual issues, finances. However, the bottom line is that most of these problems can be traced right back to false expectations. If I believe that my partner should be the perfect wife and mother—just like on some television program—it may lead to problems.

Speaking of television, where do you get your ideas about relationships? Many of them come from your family history. On the other hand, if you think about it, you may find that you get many of your ideas from the media—from television, movies, music videos, and the printed word. While some of these factors can provide positive images, often such images are distorted. People can never live up to such false expectations.

In addition, if you have been drinking or using drugs, your vision becomes even more distorted. All of those expectations you had around a "perfect partner" rise to the surface. You may find yourself engaged in battle with a partner simply because she does not meet the expectations of your fantasy, and you are not able to communicate about this when sober. You may not even be aware of why you are acting the way you are.

Think about yourself also. Have you ever had false expectations about your role as a husband, a father, or a provider? Have you ever compared yourself to some basketball celebrity and found yourself falling short? Or, have you ever compared yourself to a brother, a friend, a neighbor, or someone with whom you work? If you have done this (and who has not to an extent?), you may find that you are overly critical of yourself. You may be giving yourself bad messages: "What's the matter with me? I'll never make as much money as Mike? I'll never be as good a dad as my dad."

If you engage in this type of thinking, you may end up feeling bad about yourself. Your self-esteem may take a nose dive. You may find yourself falling into the "bad rap" trap. Instead of recognizing all the positive traits and skills that you have, you settle for putting yourself down. In turn, this can lead to anger and the build up of aggression. Eventually, you may catch yourself arguing with your wife over small things, the tension builds, emotional and verbal abuse begins, which can lead to physical abuse.

Exercise 5.8 False Expectations

1. In the space below, write a false expectation, you had about a partner.

_____

_____

_____

_____

_____

2. How did this affect your relationship? Describe the result to your group.

_____

_____

_____

_____

_____

Hands Down: A Domestic Violence Treatment Workbook

3. Now, examine false expectations you have had of yourself. Describe how this affected your attitude and behavior and any outcome with a partner.

_____

_____

_____

_____

_____

Power Struggles: If your expectations are faulty, you may end up having power struggles with your partner. Power struggles occur when you and your partner each try to win an argument. For example, you are having an argument about money. You think you are right. She thinks she is right. So, you argue back and forth. It gets louder and louder. Nobody wants to give an inch. Maybe you get the last word in.

Maybe you are the aggressive type and you bellow and threaten—or strike her—until she gives in. You think you have won. The truth is, you may have won the battle, but lost the war. Your partner is now angry with you. She may not want to talk to you for days. She gives you the silent treatment. Or, she buckles in to your demands, but inside she is seething, just waiting for a time to get revenge. You did not win anything. In fact, you probably lost—in the long run.

On the other hand, you may be a passive-aggressive person, who typically will give in during a power struggle, but then find subtle and sometimes sneaky ways of getting even or getting your way. This can be done by sulking, manipulating, or taking your anger out on others or the furniture—or dishes.

Power struggles can take many forms. Sometimes people will bring their children into this "game," trying to get the children to take sides with them against the other parent. Be aware of such tactics and stay away from them! Such controlling antics not only will destroy your relationship, but they will provide the children with mixed messages that can harm their future relationships. This also can backfire, with the children taking the other parent's side.

Exercise 5.9 Power Struggles

Think of a time you got into a power struggle with your partner and apparently gained the upper hand. Describe it. What was the final result? Who won?

_____
_____
_____
_____
_____

Enmeshment: Are you and your wife like Siamese twins? Are you inseparable? Are your lives so joined together that you can not do anything without each other? This is what is meant by *enmeshment*. All of your partner's problems are your problems, and your problems are her problems. You can not have an evening out with your friends. In other words, you have no personal identity. You are nothing without her.

In a healthy relationship, the couple remains separate individuals, but is also linked within their partnership. Everyone needs to have his or her own "space." You are individuals, even though you are a couple. You should have your own activities and your own interests. It is okay for your partner to go bowling with her team without you. It is okay for you to have a poker night without her. In fact, it is downright healthy.

Exercise 5.10 Enmeshed Relationships

1. Were you ever in an enmeshed relationship?

_____
_____
_____
_____

2. Describe why you feel it was enmeshed and how that affected any emotional, physical, or verbal abuse between you and your partner?

_____

_____

_____

_____

_____

Jealousy: This is better known as the "green-eyed monster." Sometimes jealousy can be based on reality, but most often it stems from your own fears. If you feel good about yourself and trust your partner, jealousy should not be a problem. But if you are insecure, if you are drinking or using other drugs, you may see a threat in every situation. Jealousy is closely connected to your self-esteem.

In addition, jealousy is sometimes connected with guilt. If you ever cheated on your wife, you may transfer those suspicions back to her. Maybe she has been preoccupied with something else and has not been so attentive to you lately. You remember your own cheating and perhaps have some guilty feelings. You become jealous, accusing her of cheating, when it really goes back to your own behavior.

You may believe that "jealousy is natural." Wrong. Most jealousy is unfounded. It is natural to be afraid if you think you may be losing your partner. However, if you allow unfounded jealousy to build, it is like a cancer, growing and taking control over the relationship. You may end up in verbal arguments all the time or even strike your partner in a rage. Much domestic violence occurs because of jealousy.

But remember, jealousy is not just confined to suspicions around a rival man. People can be jealous of children, work, school, friends, or activities. Perhaps you never thought of it this way. For example, take newlyweds. They are focused only on each other. Then, along comes a baby. Now, the attention is on the child. As a man, you may feel left out; you may feel that she no longer cares for you, that the baby is all she cares about. You actually become jealous of the baby!

She goes to school or work. You do not know what is going on. Even if there is no other man to worry about, the school is taking up a large part of her time. You no longer have her undivided attention. Here comes the jealousy monster again! See how this works?

Jealousy takes many forms and can be deceptive, but in a healthy relationship, it should not be present.

Exercise 5.11 Jealousy

Describe a time when you were jealous. What was the result?

_____

_____

_____

_____

_____

Cultural Influences: Some of the influences on your thinking and behavior have already been described in this unit—for example, the influences of your family system, your peers, and other relationships. Remember how those influences have affected your relationship with a partner? In addition to these factors, other messages can play a huge role in how we treat a partner.

For example, have you ever heard yourself thinking or saying any of the following:

- "Real men do not cry."
- "All women want is a paycheck."
- "The man is the head of the household."
- "Do not back down from a fight."
- "I have to be in control."

Such messages—and more—come from the world around us. Men, as well as women, hear such messages and adopt them. They come to believe them. You may have done the same thing. These messages may come from friends, from television, films, music, or the written word. The problem is, if you believe them and act upon them, they can become a part of your distorted thinking. Then, they can lead to problems in your relationship.

Think about it. If you believe that "real men do not cry," you may shut down your emotions and fail to respond when your partner and family need you the most. That can lead your partner to think you do not care. It can create tension and lack of security in the relationship.

If you believe that "I have to be in control," then you may become very angry when your wife decides to go to work. You cannot control her anymore.

Exercise 5.12 Cultural Influences

1. Read the previous list. Now, discuss with your group or a friend the ways that some of the other messages could cause bad feelings or abuse in a relationship. You may jot down any notes here:

_____
_____
_____
_____
_____

2. Read the messages again. Have you used any of them? Or, can you think of another message you have used? Write that message and then describe how it has affected your relationship.

_____
_____
_____
_____
_____

Lack of Skills: Do you know what a timeout is? Have you ever tried negotiating for something you wanted in a relationship? Do you know how to solve problems in a constructive way? Many domestic violence offenders do not have good skills in these areas. These are skills not generally taught in school. And, most people did not learn them growing up. So, how could you be expected to use them in your own family?

If you do not have good skills in areas of communication, anger management, and problem-solving, then you probably will have many more disagreements with your spouse or girlfriend. When conflicts arise, you may not know how to express your needs. When a problem occurs, you may be struggling with questions of how to fix it. Every argument may turn into a wrestling match.

In different sections of this workbook, you will learn new skills for communicating and problem solving, as well as anger management. Hopefully, you will study these techniques closely so you can use them to change from the behavior that has gotten you into trouble. In addition, other sections of this manual will provide you with some skill-building tips to help with any current or future relationship.

Exercise 5.13 Relationship Skills

What are some skills that might help you with your relationship?

_____
_____
_____
_____
_____

Building Skills

There Are No Perfect Relationships!

These five words have been put in boldface type in a special box, because they are critical. You must understand that no perfect relationship exists. If you are looking for one, you are going to be in for a rude awakening. You also will face much more stress in your relationships, because no matter who you pick for a partner, she will never live up to your expectations. **Relationships are risky.** You always are taking a chance when you fall in love. That person may not love you. Or, maybe she will leave you for someone else. Yes, there is risk involved. But the other alternative is that you will never feel the pleasure of being with someone who cares about you or the sense of joy and moments of happiness that can occur within the relationship.

Of course, you are going to have arguments. All people have disagreements. We all have different ideas and perceptions about the world in which we live. We have different values, different opinions. And that is okay. Who would want to live in a world of clones, where we all are exactly alike? Learning to support each other in spite of the differences, learning to compromise, and giving in once in a while—all are key ingredients in a healthy relationship.

All successful relationships require work. We will look at relationships compared to a plant. If I buy a beautiful, green plant and bring it home, but forget to water it, eventually it will die. Plants need healthy soil, sunlight, water, and air. Without those components, they cannot exist. Even so, we must nurture our relationships. We must provide certain elements, such as respect, stability, honesty, commitment, and trust. When we fail to provide those elements, our relationship may fade, brown out, and eventually, even the roots will die.

However, you have the ability to stop the deterioration of your relationship. Several skills can aid you in doing that. In healthy relationships, several key factors are present. Look at the house drawn below. It includes several key elements in healthy families. As you examine these, you may be able to see several areas in which you can improve.

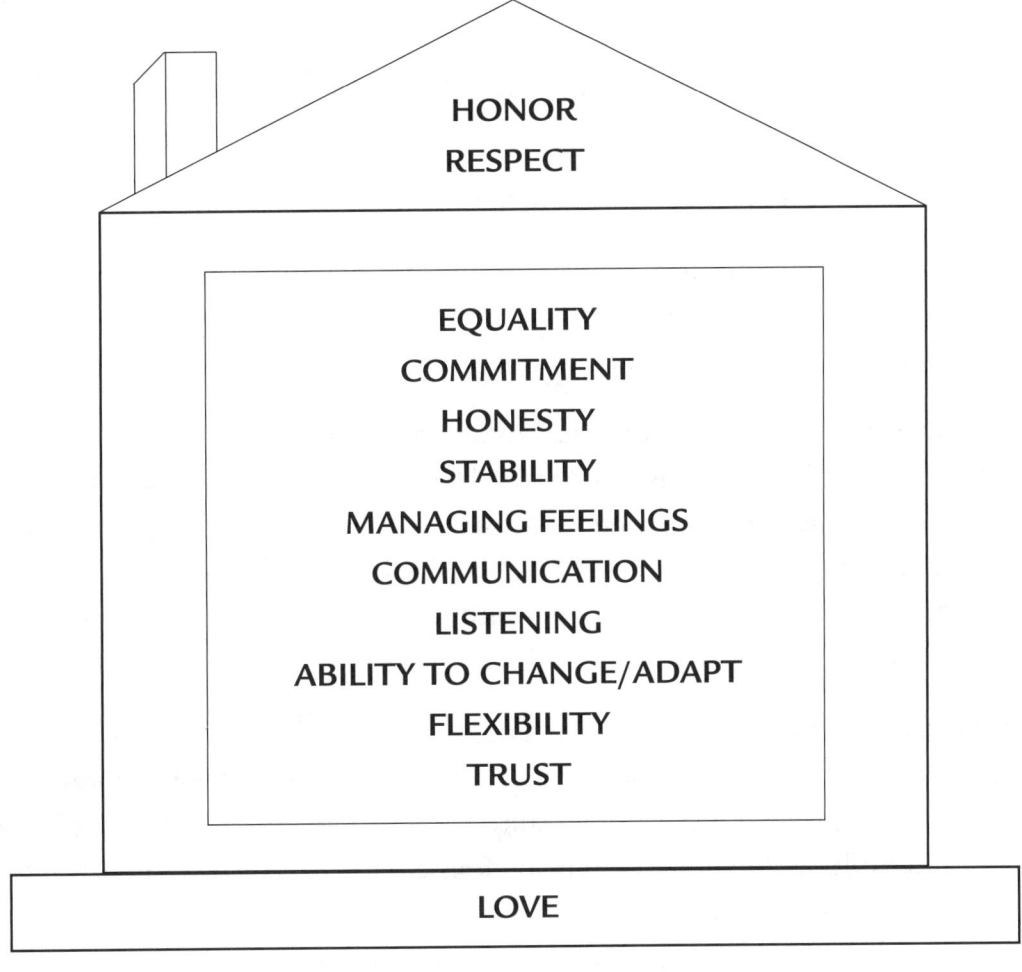

The house shows key elements in healthy families.

LOVE is at the bottom of the house because it is the **foundation** of the home. If you built a new home and did not place it on a foundation, it would start to settle. One corner might sink further into the ground. Cracks would appear in the walls. If you lived there long enough, the entire building might crumble.

The same thing can happen in a relationship without love. But what is love? You must have a good understanding of what love is before you can build a relationship on that foundation.

Exercise 5.14 Love

Quickly, write down what LOVE has meant to you in the past—your definition.

_____
_____
_____
_____
_____

How does *The Random House Webster's College Dictionary* (2001) define love?

"1. A profoundly tender, passionate affection for another person, especially when based on sexual attraction. 2. a feeling of warm personal attachment or deep affection. 3. a person to whom love is felt. 4. a love affair. 5. sexual activity...."

The list goes on through twelve other entries. No wonder love is so confusing. An entire book could be written on what love is—or is not. Instead, to keep it simple, look at this definition: "Profoundly tender . . . passionate . . . sexual attraction." Isn't that how love begins? We are attracted to another person. Call it chemistry. Call it biology. Call it spiritual. The main thing is the initial attraction. There is nothing wrong with that. That is what leads to sexual activity and keeps the human race going.

". . . warm personal attachment." Very important. ". . . deep affection." Ah ha. Now we are getting into the long-term stuff. While love starts with passion, that feeling changes with time. Some researchers say that if our bodies and brains stayed "high" on love all the time, we probably would explode! Such high intensity does create a great deal of stress. Over a period of time, the chemistry level drops. At this stage, some people decide they are not in love anymore. They do not "feel" the same. So, they go out and hunt for another person to experience the same "high" they felt with the first partner. They may repeat this pattern over and over again, throwing away partners like old clothes.

There is a tendency in our culture to confuse love with lust. This is strongly related to a desire for "instant gratification." Many people want their needs (or rather desires) fulfilled right now. Just like small children, they may throw a temper tantrum when they do not get what they want. Such behavior may include sexual partners. These people may use the word "love," but it may be just so they can enjoy a momentary sexual experience with someone. But real love—the long-term variety, the spiritual, enduring kind—goes beyond sexual feelings. It includes sex, but it also includes all of the other components listed before. After all, sex is a part of love, equality, and communicating. (What better way to communicate!) It also includes stability and respect.

Love is many things. You will need to define it for yourself. But when you do so, think about people you have known or read about, who have been there for each other through many trials, the bad times and the good. There is the wife who waits faithfully seven years while her husband is in prison. Dana Reeve stood by her husband, Christopher, after the terrible accident that left him a quadriplegic. Couples who have endured the death of a child together may have drawn strength from each other. You probably can think of some everyday partners who demonstrate this kind of devotion.

Love changes. Given time, we can discover whole new aspects of love in our relationship. But we must give it time—time to grow, to experience life together, to share the most intimate and joyous moments, as well as the pitfalls and grief. We need time to realize the spiritual aspects of love.

Love does not mean staying with someone who is emotionally, physically, or sexually abusive. That is not love. Love does not intentionally hurt others. Some people abuse their partners by trying to force them to stay in the relationship. They may stalk them, threaten them, attack them, and, in some cases, kill them. This is obsession. It is not genuine love.

"Study of a Hip Hop Artist" by BP. Media: Zine collage on recycled cardboard. Courtesy of Art Behind Bars.

Exercise 5.15 Love Revisited

A. Review the information. Think about how you would like to experience love in the future. Describe any changes in your thinking since your first definition.

_____

_____

_____

_____

_____

Honor and Respect are at the top of the house with good reason. *Honor* covers a wide range of feelings and behaviors. *The Random House Webster's College Dictionary* (2001) gives a number of meanings. For example, "high respect, as for worth, merit, or rank," "the privilege of being associated with or receiving a favor from a respected person, group, etc.," "a deferential title of respect," and "to show a courteous regard for." A judge is called "Your Honor." We also use this word when we mention the President of the United States and other important figures.

Respect is defined in the same dictionary as "esteem; admiration" and "proper acceptance or courtesy," as well as "the condition of being esteemed or honored." How do these two words apply to your relationships with your partner, children, other family members, as well as friends? Can you see how they work hand-in-hand to add to the value of a relationship?

One way that we show we care about family members and others is by giving them respect for their uniqueness and differences, even if we may not necessarily understand or agree with them (Strong, DeVault, and Sayad, 1998). Healthy families encourage the development of individuality in members, even though it can lead to differences in opinions.

Honoring and respecting people in our lives means we need to be there for them and listen to their needs. Think about how you may have taken your partner for granted in the past. Maybe you just assumed she would always be there while you may have been busy all day—working, taking care of business and chores. Sometimes it seems like there is little time to stop and just talk. However, honoring your partner means taking the time. Healthy relationships demonstrate strong commitment (Strong, DeVault, and Sayad, 1998).

When you have a disagreement, have you ever stopped and thought about just listening, even if you did not agree with her? Do you take into consideration her point of view? Respect means listening, hearing the other person out. It is part of communication and goes hand-in-hand with love. It means that you treat the other person with consideration. You listen when she has a complaint. And then, you try to talk through disagreements and reach a compromise.

If you honor your partner, you will make a greater effort to make your marriage work. Some marriage counselors believe that honor is the cornerstone of the marriage. You might think of this in another way, too. If you honor your work, you will do a better job. No matter how menial or trivial it may be, you will do it to the best of your ability. This is true of almost any situation or person and goes back to the idea of commitment or willingness to work for the continuity and well-being of the relationship.

On the other hand, some men grumble about being "disrespected," saying things like "no one's going to disrespect me like that." And they may hint at attacking the other person, forcing her "respect." Some parents even do this with their children. However, respect cannot be forced. It is earned. It is a part of honor. What these people are really talking about is fear. Generally speaking, if the other person buckles in to their demands, that person does it out of fear. This is not true respect.

Exercise 5.16 Respect

1. Recall a time when you tried to force your partner to respect you. Perhaps you demanded it. Describe the event and what the result was. Be prepared to discuss this event with your group.

_____
_____
_____
_____

2. Is there another way you could have handled the situation? Describe it and how it might have changed the outcome of the situation.

_____
_____
_____
_____

Equality. Within the walls of the house are other items—all important to maintaining a healthy relationship. First, you will find **Equality**. Equality means that both partners in a relationship should be treated equally. No one should be "the boss." Both need to be consulted for important decisions, such as making purchases, making job changes, choosing housing, and disciplining children. In other words, this includes any matters in which you both have an interest. Equality means that you ask, not demand. Both you and your partner need to be involved in disciplining the children. You both need to share household chores in an agreeable and fair manner. You need to compromise when disagreements occur. The key word is "sharing."

One common error states that relationships should be 50/50. This is a myth. In healthy relationships, a person may have to give up 100 percent in one situation, but gain 75 percent in another. In other words, you do not keep count. You do what is important and valuable in keeping the relationship working. You do not try to keep your trade-offs equal. For example, stating, "I let you watch the Oscars last night, now I'm entitled to two hours of my choice tonight."

Think back to your relationships. Did you ever treat your partner like a servant? Did you insist on making all the important decisions? Did you refuse to do the dishes because that's "woman's work"? And did you ever prevent your partner from getting a job or going to school? If you did any of these things, you were using power and control tactics. Relationships founded on power and control are like a volcano. The magma under the surface continues to heat and build; eventually, there is an explosion. You may find that ideas of equality are foolish. You may be saying to yourself that your parents were not worried about such nonsense. But if your past relationships fell apart, you may want to examine your own thinking and behavior. Do you truly believe in equality? Or, do you just pretend when it suits your purpose?

Exercise 5.17 Equality

Read the following sentences and fill in the blanks from the above information or your own experience.

1. When both partners treat each other with respect and consult each other on mutual decisions, this is called _____.

2. The care of the children should belong to _____.

3. Repair and fixing of the car should belong to _____.

4. _____ should be the boss in the family.

5. When disagreements occur in a relationship, the couple should seek to _____.

6. Preventing a partner from going back to college is an example of _____ and _____ tactics.

Commitment is another important skill in maintaining healthy relationships. Commitment includes sticking together through bad times and good times. It means not giving up when you argue about money, sex, or the kids. Commitment is a major factor in love. People who are committed do not just stay together because of the wedding vows. They stay together because they care and understand that sometimes the journey is difficult. Since we are all human, we sometimes are going to make mistakes. Have you ever said something you were sorry for later? Have you ever done something you regretted later? Of course you have. But, in a healthy relationship, people forgive each other. They are there for each other. You can call your spouse if you lock your keys in the car, and she will bring you the extra set. In other words, you can count on her.

Exercise 5.18 Commitment

Has your partner been able to count on you? Why or why not?

_____
_____
_____
_____

Stability goes along with commitment. In fact, if you review the qualities listed inside the house, you will find that they overlap. They are connected. Stability refers to several things. First of all, the family keeps a fairly structured routine. They get up at about the same time, send kids off to school, go to work, eat meals at certain times, and have set bedtimes. During the week, they have specific activities. This type of routine is very important to children. It produces a sense of security within them.

Stability also includes providing basic needs for the family. Basic needs include housing, food, clothing, and heat. Those are key elements that everyone needs to survive. But other needs may include such items as education, safety, health, social activities, and spiritual qualities.

If you spent a large portion of your income on drugs or alcohol, that reduces the stability of your family system. If you failed to help your children learn to brush their teeth or shower, this takes away from stability. Refer back to the chaotic family system discussed earlier to get a solid idea of what stability is not.

Exercise 5.19 Stability

In what other ways do families show stability?

_____
_____
_____
_____
_____

Managing Feelings is another key factor in relationships. Managing your feelings first requires that you learn to recognize your feelings—whether you are angry, happy, disappointed, or joyous. These are all human emotions. But if you have been using drugs and drinking excessively, you may have a hard time experiencing real emotions. It may take several weeks, even months of being sober and clean, before you can experience a natural "high." Some people are fearful of their feelings. They do not know how to deal with them, so they may use a substance to cope with them.

Secondly, you need to accept your feelings—good and bad. You do not have to act on them. Just because you have a certain feeling does not mean you have to follow through. For example, you are angry with your wife for spending too much money on clothes. Anger is your feeling (refer to Chapter 7: Anger, Stress, and Domestic Violence). However, you do not have to scream and yell or assault her. There are other ways to handle your feelings.

Finally, you can learn some ways to manage your anger, frustrations, and disappointments. All these emotions will occur as you go through life. You can learn these skills in a class, talking with a counselor, or reading a book. You may get some help by talking to a friend and getting some tips. In addition, managing feelings is closely connected to communicating, which was discussed in Chapter 5.

What happens if you cannot manage feelings in your relationship? Have you ever gotten angry at your spouse and gone to work? Perhaps you found yourself yelling at a coworker or your boss. This is called *displaced anger*. This type of anger can result in poor productivity on the job—or even get you fired.

Or, maybe you have let your anger build up over a period of time, and one day your spouse wants to go to lunch with her friend, and you explode. You call her "a bitch" and threaten to take the kids away. Anger will come out—in one way or another. You may experience it inwardly and develop high blood pressure or other physical problems, or outwardly, by yelling, screaming, and assaulting others.

Here is another scenario: You have a hard time expressing feelings, so you rarely tell your wife and children that you love them. You never praise or thank them for doing chores. You use the "silent treatment," refusing to talk or process your feelings. How do you think this makes your family feel? How do you think this might affect the outcome of the marriage?

Exercise 5.20 Managing Feelings

A. True or False

Respond to these statements with either "T" for true or "F" for "false," and then discuss them with the group.

_____ 1. Some people use alcohol to mask their feelings.

_____ 2. The first step in managing feelings is to develop skills.

_____ 3. Anger management is one tool that can help with feelings.

_____ 4. Anger can build up and cause a person to explode at some point.

_____ 5. I do not need to accept my feelings or recognize them to successfully manage them.

_____ 6. Good communication skills can help manage feelings.

_____ 7. Feelings and behavior are the same thing.

B. Describe any trouble you have had expressing your feelings. Why do you think this was hard for you?

_____

_____

_____

_____

_____

Healthy communication involves many different areas—not just talking. People can talk for hours and say nothing. Think about a family sitting around the table, having a disagreement. Dad wants to buy a poker table with their tax refund. Mom wants to get a new washer. Sis wants to take a trip to Vegas with her friends. And brother wants to put it into a car. They each argue to get his or her own way. Soon, the argument turns to name-calling. They begin putting each other down, whining and threatening. Finally, father stands up, knocks the table over, and says, "I'm in charge here! What I say goes!" Is this healthy communication? Of course not. Sometimes it is not what you say, but how you say it that makes the difference.

There are many types of communication. You may want to refer to Chapter 5: "Communication" in this workbook. Remember, **listening** is a key ingredient in healthy communication. Many people are great at talking—rattling on and on. But when it comes to letting another person talk and stopping to listen, that is something else.

Do you really hear what the other person has to say, sometimes "reading between the lines"? For example, you ask your wife, "How are you doing today?" She says, "Fine," but you see her eyes are downcast, and she has a frown on her face. You should know something is wrong. She may be sick, angry, or worried. Body language is at work. It is an extremely important part of communication.

Consider why communication is so important in relationships. Without good communication, people are going to misunderstand each other. They may get mixed messages or withhold information from each other. This creates conflict, which can lead to domestic violence.

Exercise 5.21 Communication

1. Name one area that you had trouble communicating in your relationship. Why do you think this happened?

_____

_____

_____

_____

_____

2. Can you think of any way to change the situation and improve your communication?

_____

_____

_____

_____

_____

The ability to change or adapt is critical to successful family systems. Situations and circumstances are always changing in the family. Think about it. Having a child is a huge change in the family and in the relationship of the couple. If the couple does not successfully adapt to this change, they may end up divorced. Other changes might include changing your job, moving across town or to another city or state, one person going to school, changing finances (up or down), going to prison, being ill or having a disease, or dying.

All of these events can occur as you move through life. Sometimes the events are not so dramatic—a child growing up, maturing, going on her first date, a child learning to drive. The TV burns out. The car requires new tires. The plumbing backs up in the house. Of course, all of these events produce stress. But if you cannot accept them as they occur, and then determine how to handle them, the stress may spill out and damage your marriage.

Closely related to the ability to change or adapt, is **flexibility**. Flexibility is defined as being easily bent or adaptable. Remember the healthy, flexible family system? This implies that while stability is important, the ability to make choices in individual situations is critical. Flexibility goes along with the ability to change. A couple who has no flexibility will fall apart when change occurs.

A couple went to marriage counseling. Both worked outside the home. The wife was seeking greater communication from her husband and also wanting him to help more with chores. After about three sessions, he spoke up and insisted, "She knew who I was when I married her. I'm never going to change!" Needless to say, this couple divorced within a year.

Exercise 5.22 Flexibility

How do you handle change? Can you adapt when unexpected situations arise? Recall an event where a change suddenly occurred in your life. Describe how you handled it.

_____
_____
_____
_____

Finally, we will examine the idea of **Trust.** In a healthy relationship, partners trust each other. They allow the other person to have privacy and freedom. They respect one another's individual boundaries. Their partner can take a class at the local community college without being accused of cheating. The partner can spend an evening with friends without jealousy rearing its head. They believe the other person is being faithful and have confidence that the relationship will grow. Doubt, fear, suspicion—these have no place in a relationship built on trust.

Think of a relationship like a bank account. If you put money into the account, it will grow and perhaps even gain interest. If you continue to take money out, or worse, take more out than you put in, eventually the bank will close your account. You even may owe the bank money. How does this work between partners? Look at the following chart:

DEPOSITS	WITHDRAWALS
Helping with dishes	Reading the paper while she does chores
Taking her to a movie	Refusing to go to "chick flicks" with her
Praising her to a friend	Putting her cooking/childcare down
Remaining faithful	Having an affair
Bringing flowers for no reason	Forgetting important dates, anniversary

Exercise 5.23 Trust

What is your relationship balance? Look at the prior list. Perhaps you even can think of other ways to increase your account. Discuss this with your group. What other ways do you decrease the balance?

_____

_____

_____

_____

Effect of Violence on Children

Think back to when you were a child. What are the earliest memories of your parents? Did you come from a family where there was a lot of screaming, yelling, and fighting? If so, look back in this section and recall how learned behavior may have affected your current actions. Now, think about how such violence may have affected your children. If you do not have children at this time, perhaps you will in the future. Perhaps you have nephews or nieces, friends with children, or your girlfriend has children—these are all kids whose lives can be affected by violence.

Just how are children impacted by violence? Researchers have conducted many studies in this area. Some have been on children living in shelters with their mothers. Others have studied adults who describe their past childhood experiences. And they all come up with similar results.

Children in violent homes suffer from many reactions. For example, they may:

- Feel responsible for the abuse
- Feel guilty for not being able to stop the abuse
- Be afraid that they are going to be hurt
- Be embarrassed to bring friends home
- Have constant anxiety or suffer posttraumatic stress disorder
- Have eating or sleeping disorders

- Revert to bed-wetting, nail-biting, and other habits
- Have problems in school
- Be sick a lot more than usual
- Get into many fights or withdraw from conflict
- Become suicidal or homicidal

We will examine some of these factors. It might seem strange to you that children would feel guilty or responsible for the situation. But a child does not think like an adult. Picture this scene. You are in the living room, playing with your toys. Mom is in the kitchen cooking supper, and father walks in the door. Your toys are scattered all over the living room. Dad kicks a Tonka truck lying in his path, as he makes his way to the kitchen.

"Where in the hell is your mother?" he yells. And then, seeing her, "Why isn't supper on the table? You know I've got ball practice tonight! And what's this crap doing all over the floor? Don't you do anything but watch soap operas all day?" And with that, he kicks over the Lego castle you worked on for hours.

Now the fight is on. You slink into a corner. And you think to yourself, *If I had picked up my toys, they would not be fighting. It's all my fault.*

To an adult, that may be illogical, but to a child it makes perfect sense. In fact, the child may carry that thinking over into adulthood and blame himself whenever things go wrong at home, at work, or at play.

In addition, the child may be afraid of getting hurt. He watches dad shove mom against the cabinet, and she strikes her arm, drawing blood. She is holding it at an awkward angle, moaning in pain. Picture yourself again as that child, drawing back in fear. Maybe you even will slink into your room, out of the line of fire.

You may have another fear as you retreat. You may be afraid that your mother will die, that she will be taken from you, and you will be taken out of the home. Maybe this has happened before. You remember the police banging on the door, and mom trying to tell them it was okay. You remember that they took you away one night, and you had to stay with strangers for a week. Now, you lay in bed late at night, shaking and crying yourself to sleep.

Such fears and anxiety can lead even very small children to suffer from posttraumatic stress disorder. Posttraumatic stress disorder originally was known as "shell-shock." Veterans coming home from war would have horrible nightmares and flashbacks. They were startled easily, and showed high levels of anxiety and nervousness, an inability to concentrate, and were quite jumpy. Studies later found that people do not have to go to war to have these same symptoms. Anyone who is traumatized can have them. Rape victims often exhibit these symptoms. People who have been severely beaten or those who have gone through some terrible event and survived, such as the World Trade Center tragedy may have them. People, who are abused, such as domestic violence victims, may show such symptoms. Finally, children who grow up in homes with domestic violence also can develop posttraumatic stress disorder. For these children, the home becomes a war zone.

As a result of living with domestic violence, the child may have increased risks, such as behavioral, social, and emotional problems, as well as cognitive and attitudinal problems (Carlson, 2000; Edleson, 1999; Rossman, 2001, in National Clearinghouse on Child Abuse and Neglect Information). For example, even though a child has been potty- trained, he may go back to soiling himself. He may begin biting his nails, pulling at his hair, or wetting the bed. Some children develop aggressive behavior, hitting and biting other children. Some become very shy, hiding out in the safety of their room. Some children may be sick a lot, have stomachaches, headaches, leg pains—a variety of symptoms with no real physical cause. They may begin to miss school, and their grades may start falling off. Eventually, they may drop out.

How would you feel if your parents were fighting all the time and if you never knew what was going to happen when you opened the door to your house? Maybe mom has a black eye or a broken arm. Would you want to explain this to your friends?

At some point, the child may start using alcohol and/or other drugs to cope with the problems at home. In addition, he may be highly stressed, overanxious, and may be diagnosed with a condition such as attention deficit hyperactivity disorder (ADHD). This condition includes a variety of symptoms. For example, the child may be very nervous, unable to concentrate on school work, constantly seeking attention, and be unable to sit still (Bernstein, Clarke-Stewart, Roy, Srull, and Wickens, 1994). This does not mean he is hyperactive, but he certainly should be checked. However, he may be reacting to the conflict in the home. Severe stress and trauma can lead to changes in brain chemistry.

Eventually, if one parent continues to abuse the other, a child can begin to think that life would be better if the abusive parent were dead. There are many cases on record where a child has attempted to kill an abusive parent and, in some cases, succeeded.

As you can see, a child raised in a home filled with domestic violence can suffer severe emotional and behavioral trauma. Even if you think the children are in another room, sound asleep in their beds, you are wrong. They are listening. They are learning.

Exercise 5.24 Effect of Violence on Children

1. If you were raised in a home with domestic violence, what type of violence do you recall? Was it emotional, verbal, physical, or sexual?

_____

_____

_____

2. Describe the type of situation and what thoughts went thorough your mind when your parents were arguing or fighting.

_____

_____

_____

_____

_____

3. If you were not raised in such a home, try to imagine that you are a child in a situation involving domestic violence. What thoughts would go through your mind?

_____

_____

_____

_____

4. What did you do (or would you do) when your parents were fighting?

_____

_____

_____

_____

5. Now, think about your own children (or your relatives' or friends' children). How do you think they feel when you and your partner are arguing, calling each other names, screaming, yelling, or shoving each other?

___
___
___
___
___

Exercise 5.25 Your Role as a Parent

As an introduction to this section, write down some of the key things that children need to develop emotionally and physically.

___
___
___
___
___

Now, discuss your answers with your group and facilitator.

You probably had a number of excellent suggestions. Compare your answers and those of your group with the following information. First, examine the picture on the next page.

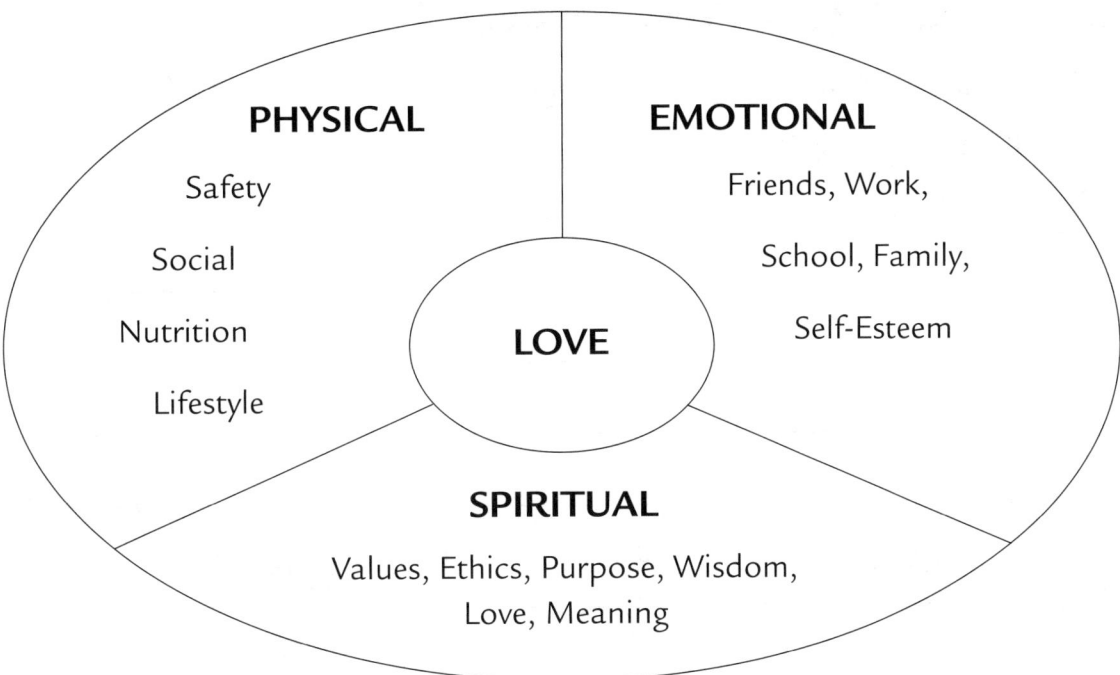

Needs of Healthy People

The circle above shows three basic areas that all of us, including our children, need in order to be healthy. The centerpiece is **LOVE.** Love spills over into the other three areas, and should be the primary motivation that controls the other three areas. If a parent truly loves his child, then all of his actions and behaviors should reflect that. The lessons he teaches his child will reflect his love. For example, if your child falls down and cuts his knee, a hug demonstrates you care. It shows your love. However, if you yell at your child, "You clumsy idiot! Why don't you watch where you're going?" the child gets another message, and it is not one of love.

Surrounding love in this diagram are the physical, emotional, and spiritual components. Under each area are several elements. Some of these may have been listed in your prior exercise. We will examine them in more detail.

PHYSICAL: Safety is critical. The child needs to be protected from things that might hurt her. For example, household cleaning products should be kept locked up or out of her reach. Remove all dangling cords, hide open electric plugs, and gate the stairs and dangerous areas. These things are all are very important in maintaining safety.

Exercise 5.26: Safety Concerns for Parents

1. Think of other safety tips for parents with children. Write several other safety tips to share with the other participants.

_____
_____
_____
_____
_____

2. What about parents who use alcohol or drugs around their children? Do you think this could present safety problems for the child? How?

_____
_____
_____
_____
_____

3. What about parents who manufacture or make drugs in the presence of their children?

_____
_____
_____
_____
_____

4. In some states, parents and other adults can be charged with child abuse (as well as other charges) if they are making a drug, such as methamphetamine, with a child present. Children have been injured and killed in these situations. Of course, such children can be taken from the home and placed in foster care. In addition, such parents are training their children to be drug manufacturers, users, and breakers of the law. In other words, they are very poor role models for their children.

Nutrition and fitness fall under the physical area. The parents' responsibility in this area includes teaching your children to eat a healthy diet that includes fruits and vegetables, along with whole grains. Does this mean your kid can never have a soda or a candy bar? Of course it does not. But some children today seem to be raised on fast food. Some turn up their noses at an orange or a salad. As a result, too many of our children are overweight. So, to keep them healthy, it is important that we teach them early. This includes getting exercise—walking, running, jumping rope, swimming, bicycling. Setting an example by playing and exercising with your children is especially useful.

Social activities are also very important in the overall well-being of a child. Learning to play with other children, to participate in activities, as well as watch, gives a child a head start in the emotional arena as well. This can make a child develop good self-esteem and to learn to solve problems with others in the world.

The right thing. You might be saying to yourself, "This all sounds good, but I'm not with her mother. I'm not sending any money because I do not know if her mother will spend it on my daughter or herself!" You are right. You do not know. But ask yourself, what is the right thing to do? You can not control what your ex does, but you can control what you do.

Exercise 5.27 Activities for Children

1. Did you teach your child to brush his teeth? To take a shower? How about providing clothing, shoes, and other essentials? Make a list of the things that you shared with your child or another child.

_____

_____

_____

_____

2. Now, list the items you failed to share.

_____

_____

_____

_____

_____

The spiritual area includes helping your children to develop a sense of themselves—who they are, what their purpose on planet earth is, and why they exist. These are "big" questions that we adults continue to ask ourselves throughout our lives. But it is essential that we start our children on this quest. Some people use formal religion to help their children develop these ideas, as well as define their morals and values. Religion can be a very positive method to achieve these goals. However, other people use a less formal approach, but focus on values and ethics.

Spiritual issues also can include discipline. After all, this is where your child can learn what is "good" behavior or "bad" behavior. Just telling them often is not enough. For example, if you want your child to learn to teach others in a nonviolent manner, then it is critical that you demonstrate that behavior to your child. If you are bullying others, threatening your wife, and slamming doors, chances are your child will do as you do, not as you say. As a parent, you sometimes must and should discipline—but remember this should be healthy discipline, not harsh punishment. It should be logical, clear, and consistent.

Exercise 5.28 Spiritual Development

1. Think about your own spiritual development. What ideas did you get in your family about religion or spirituality while growing up?

_____

_____

_____

_____

_____

2. Now, consider your own children. What values have you tried to pass on to them? If you have not had contact with your children or do not have children, list the values you would like to pass on.

_____

_____

_____

_____

_____

Emotional development also covers the physical and spiritual components. Feeling is a part of every area of your life. It overlaps everything. However, it can be broken into several parts. How children feel about themselves, school, friends, family, and later work—all fit into their development. And you, as a parent, play a huge role in helping your children to develop their self-esteem. Self-esteem can provide them with motivation and the ability to get along well with others. It can give them the desire to perform well in school or to achieve a specific career goal.

Emotional development also includes providing encouragement and support for your child. How do you respond if your child wants to play a flute in the school band? Do you tell him that it is a "girl's" instrument? Do you tell him he needs to be on the football team and quit thinking about that stupid band? Or, do you realize that he may have a special talent and rent a flute for the semester?

Emotional development means giving affection, that includes hugs and kisses, and listening when your son does not get invited on the camping trip, or drying your daughter's tears when her first boyfriend "dumps" her. It means letting your child make mistakes—because he will. We all do. It means being patient when you are at your wit's end and dead tired at the end of the day and your three-year-old comes in and begs, "Read me a story, Daddy," and you really do not want to. But you do, because that is what good parenting is all about.

Remember, how your child sees the world, how she sees other people, how she sees marriage and relationships between people—all of this can go back to how you parent your child or the child in your life.

Exercise 5.29 Emotional Development

1. Can you remember a time when you were discouraged by a parent or caretaker? Briefly describe it and your feelings.

_____
_____
_____
_____
_____

2. Describe a time when you may have wounded your child or another child emotionally. How do you feel about that now?

_____
_____
_____
_____
_____

Victim-Perpetrator Roles

You might be thinking, "What does all this have to do with domestic violence?" If you are abusing your spouse, whether you are together or separated—whether you are abusing her physical, emotionally, or sexually—your child knows. And if you are doing this, then you are not meeting the emotional, physical, and spiritual needs of your child. Even if you are providing clothing for your child, you are not meeting the child's foremost needs, if you are teaching him to abuse or be abused.

Remember earlier when we talked about learned behavior. Just to repeat, children in homes where domestic violence is present typically learn to be either perpetrators or victims. This does not mean that they are doomed and must repeat that behavior. But it does mean that it happens much too often. Again, people can break those patterns, but it requires genuine desire and hard work.

However, as a parent, you should not want to set your child up to live the same unhealthy patterns that you have been living. You should not be committing acts of violence in the first place—and certainly not in the presence of children. Again, do not say, "They do not know. They were asleep." It is just not true. They do know, and they do suffer.

Exercise 5.30 Victim-Perpetrator

1. If you could apologize to your child for committing violent acts in his or her presence, what would you say?

_____

_____

_____

_____

_____

Read the poem, *Children Learn What They Live*, attributed to Dorothy L. Nolte, on the next page. After you have read the poem, discuss what it means and how it pertains to domestic violence with your group.

Children Learn What They Live*

If children live with criticism,
    they learn to condemn.
If children live with hostility,
    they learn to fight.
If children liven with fear,
    they learn to be apprehensive.
If children live with pity,
    they learn to feel sorry for themselves.
If children live with ridicule,
    they learn to be shy.
If children live with jealousy,
    they learn what envy is.
If children live with shame,
    they learn to feel guilty.
If children live with tolerance,
    they learn to be patient.
If children live with encouragement,
    they learn to be confident.
If children live with praise,
    they learn to appreciate.
If children live with approval,
    they learn to like themselves.
If children live with acceptance,
    they learn to find love in the world.
If children live with recognition,
    they learn to have a goal.
If children live with sharing,
    they learn to be generous.
If children live with honesty and fairness,
    they learn what truth and justice are.
If children live with security,
    they learn to have faith in themselves and in those around them.
If children live with friendliness,
    they learn that the world is a nice place in which to live.
If children live with serenity,
    They learn to have peace of mind.

* Excerpted from the book *Children Learn What They Live,* Copyright © 1998 by Dorothy Law Nolte and Rachel Harris, from the poem "Children Learn What They Live," copyright © 1972 by Dorothy Law Nolte. Used by permission of Workman Publishing Co., Inc., New York. All Rights Reserved.

How are your children living?

Other Victims

At the beginning of this section, we listed several types of relationships. Remember, many different people are affected by your behavior. Often, the tendency is to think that only the person you verbally, physically, or sexually abused is the victim. Forget that. As just shown, children are primary examples of that crooked thinking.

Think of your victims as either direct victims or indirect victims. This is just what the term implies. For example, a direct victim would be the wife you struck, just as the direct victim of a robbery would be the person whose purse you snatched. An indirect victim, on the other hand, would include anyone else who might be affected by your behavior. This could be your parents who are embarrassed by your behavior and arrest. It might be your boss, who was depending on you to show up for work on Monday, but now you are sitting in jail.

Exercise 5.31 Other Victims

1. List the direct victims of any domestic violence incident and then list the indirect victims.

Direct Victims   **Indirect Victims**

_____   _____

_____   _____

_____   _____

_____   _____

2. Briefly state how these victims have been affected. Try to put yourself in their shoes.

_____

_____

_____

_____

_____

3. Finally, answer the following question:

Who is responsible for the violence I used in any relationship?

_____

Chapter 6: Anger, Stress, and Domestic Violence

(3–4 Sessions)

Objectives

▶ To examine personal patterns of anger

▶ To recognize personal anger triggers

▶ To learn to use anger-management tools effectively

▶ To recognize "bad" stress

▶ To develop healthy ways of handling stress

▶ To further develop responsibility for controlling anger

Relationship of Anger, Stress, and Domestic Violence

To better understand the relationship of anger and stress to domestic violence, it is important to understand what anger and stress mean. Have you ever said, "I can't control myself when I get angry?" Or "I'm so stressed, I'm ready to explode?" Or "She made me so angry, I couldn't help myself." So, just what is this stuff called "anger?"

Definitions

Anger: An emotion. "A strong feeling of displeasure and belligerence aroused by a real or supposed wrong" (*Random House Webster's College Dictionary*, 2001). A key to understanding this is to realize that anger and behavior are not the same. Anger is an emotion. The behavior is what you choose to do with the anger. There can be many levels of anger. Anger can be mild, moderate, or intense (rage, for example).

Stress: The dictionary defines stress as "a specific response by the body to a stimulus as fear of pain that disturbs or interferes with the normal physiological [physical] equilibrium [balance]" or "physical, mental, or emotional strain or tension"(*Random House Webster's College Dictionary*, 2001). Think about this. When you are stressed, you are thrown off balance. You may experience physical pain, such as a headache, or you may find yourself yelling at someone for no good reason.

Anger and stress are like brothers. They are so closely related that it is often difficult to tell where one starts in and the other leaves off. Which comes first—the anger or the stress? Sometimes you may have been stressed about finances, work, or some other situation and that led to anger. At other times, your anger over a situation may have contributed to more stress. These two feelings get linked together to create strong feelings and the potential for poor choices and bad behavior.

But wait! Are anger and stress all bad or negative? We will look at that idea.

Positive and Negative Aspects of Stress and Anger

Not all anger and stress is bad. Anger can lead a person to take action, even positive action. For example, several years ago, a lady in California got enraged. Her thirteen-year-old daughter had been killed by a drunken driver who had a long history of drunk driving. He was still driving on a legitimate license. She said to herself that this was wrong, and she told other people, and even took it to the legislature. This grassroots effort led to changes in the California law and even the laws of most other states. Her name is Candy Lightener, and she started MADD (Mothers Against Drunk Driving).

There are many other examples throughout history of people who got angry and did something about it. But think of your own life, your own community. Any person who gets angry because of an injustice or wrong and stands up to fight demonstrates how anger can work for the good.

In addition, anger is like a traffic signal. Green--go; red--stop; yellow--caution, be careful. Try to think of it that way. Yes, I am angry about the way that my cellmate looked at me today. Do I "go," threaten him, even strike him? Do I "stop," back away, get out of the line of fire? Do I use "caution," carefully consider my options? Anger offers us that choice BEFORE we make a decision.

Role of Self-Esteem and Impulse Control: A person with high or positive self-esteem may not feel very threatened when someone looks at him a certain way. This does not mean he is not cautious (especially in a prison environment), but rather that he has stopped and is considering the consequences to himself and others before making a decision. At times in life, people have to protect their bodies and lives. The point here is that people who feel good about themselves do not need to go around threatening others and being bullies. They know how to use, but not abuse, the power and control tactics discussed in the relationship unit.

In addition, people with poor self-esteem often have trouble with impulse control. They do not seem to be able to control their feelings; they just explode. They are often in a rage; almost anything sets them off. Some of these people may have mental health conditions and should consider getting an evaluation by a trained professional. But usually, such behaviors are learned, and (here's the good news) they can be unlearned with hard work.

Exercise 6.1 Stress and Anger

Using a scale from 1-10 (with 10 being the highest level of anger), rate one incident in your life where stress and anger came together to cause you to act in a manner not in your best interest. Now, describe it.

_____

_____

_____

_____

_____

_____

Models of Anger

Cycle of Violence: The Cycle of Violence was first proposed by a psychologist, Lenore Walker, who has done extensive work with female victims. The model looks like this:

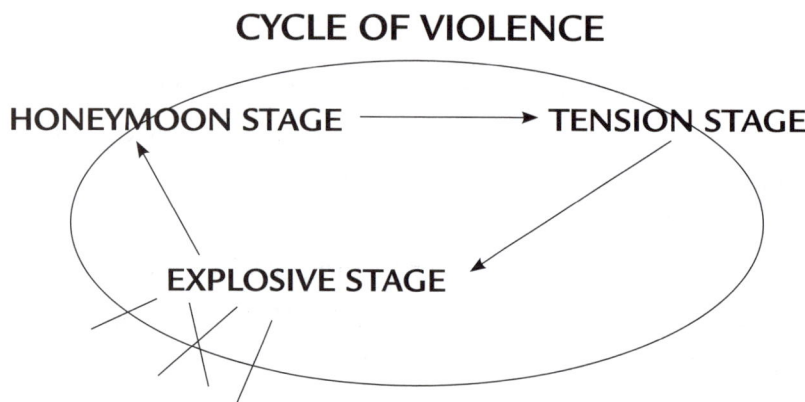

Walker proposed that in a relationship, the stress may begin with the Tension-Building Stage. This is where people may nitpick at each other and some name calling occurs. They may throw in some sarcasm. Then, the behavior escalates. The nasty behavior becomes more and more frequent and more intense, louder, and more hateful, until finally it results in the Explosive Stage. This stage is usually much shorter. At this stage, someone may get hit, the police may be called, or the victim may be taken to the hospital.

The final stage is the Honeymoon Stage, sometimes known as "Hearts and Flowers." At this time, the perpetrator will tell the victim, "I'm so sorry. It will never happen again. I swear." The victim sees the good side of the relationship and has hope. She may tell herself, "He didn't mean it. He really is trying to do better. He says he'll go to counseling now." This hope is one factor, which keeps the victim in the relationship—sometimes far too long for her own safety.

However, as Walker points out, if the perpetrator is not sincere, if he has not gotten help, if no intervention has occurred, then the cycle will start all over again. And, unfortunately, in some cases, eventually the Honeymoon Stage will drop off. The couple will go from tension building to explosion back to tension building, over and over.

How can this cycle be stopped? It can be stopped by intervention—either at some point in the Tension-Building Stage, when the victim says "enough" and has the courage to leave or get help. It can occur following the Explosion Stage when the victim does not buy into the Honeymoon Stage and remains separated from the perpetrator. It will not occur in the Honeymoon Stage unless the victim has become very self-aware and aware of the controlling tactics used in the Honeymoon Stage. At this stage, the perpetrator has not gotten his way by his tension tactics, so now he is being very, very nice. It is still a method of control.

If you are aware of your behavior in this cycle, you can make a choice to act differently. That is the point of this course, you have a choice in how you behave. In the long run, this cycle of violence does not benefit you. You are in this course because of your behavior up till now. You are here to learn a new approach.

Anger Model: The second model looks like this:

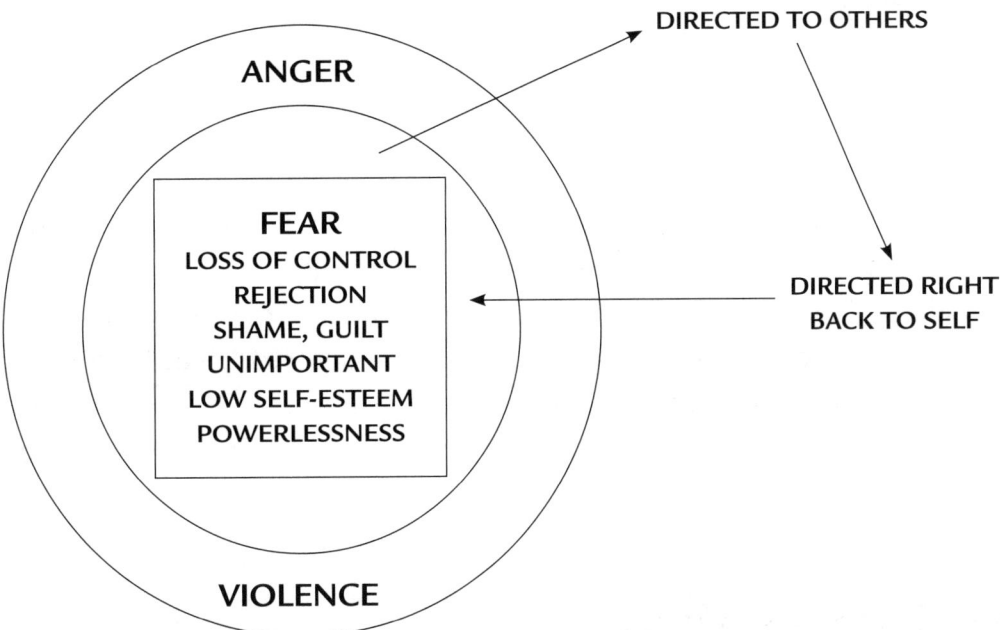

What this model indicates is that fear is at the heart of anger. Anger and its accompanying behavior, violence, is just a thin shell on the outer edge, similar to those M&Ms with thin shells covering the chocolate core. Under this shell lies specific fears, such as those listed above. Or, you may have another fear that is not included in the brief list. These fears drive the anger and push it out toward other people. In turn, the anger is then directed back toward yourself, where it grows and gets more intense and eventually leads to an explosion. This model explains why counselors tell you that anger is a secondary emotion. In other words, there is always something beneath the anger that is driving it.

The Chain Model: This model is often used in treatment to explain how behaviors, feelings, and actions are linked. For example:

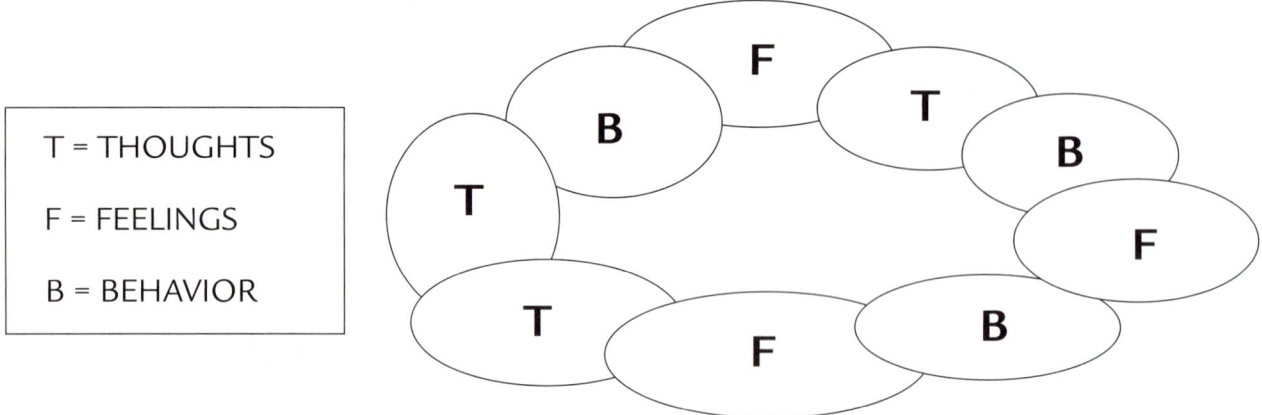

T = THOUGHTS

F = FEELINGS

B = BEHAVIOR

What this model primarily shows is that it does not matter what occurs first. You can have the thought first, followed by a feeling, and then an action. Or, you might have the feeling, followed by a thought, and then the action. Or, an action might occur first, which triggers thoughts and feelings. The point is that thoughts, feelings, and anger are all directly linked. In other words, when you catch yourself having certain thoughts, such as "Just wait. I'll get even," then, you can examine those thoughts and take a positive action. In other words, you can change your behavior. You may not be able to change your feelings at the moment, but you can change your self-talk and your choices.

Exercise 6.2 Anger Model

Examine the second Anger Model and describe what fears have driven your anger in the past and which drive your anger now.

_____
_____
_____
_____
_____
_____
_____

Hands Down: A Domestic Violence Treatment Workbook

Recognizing Your Anger

How do you know when you are angry? Have you ever gotten out of control, maybe beat someone up, and later said, "I didn't mean to do it. I got so mad, I just couldn't stop myself!" You were probably making an excuse for your bad behavior. However, it is also true that some people are so used to avoiding their angry feelings and not dealing with them, that they do not recognize when they are angry. Anger is like a mountain. At the bottom of the mountain are feelings such as irritation and frustration. They are a low-level form of anger, and, if not handled, can lead to the top of the mountain—rage. At the bottom of the mountain, you can stop yourself, if you become self-aware. However, once you start up that mountain, and your body chemicals begin to flow, it is difficult to stop. That is why it is important to recognize anger at an early stage.

We will start by examining different personality types and see how they handle their anger. Identify which type you are most like.

Passive (Stuffed) Anger: Passive people are generally very quiet. They are shy, often fearful about speaking up. They get very uncomfortable when situations get loud or aggressive. Often, they become victims, as they have a hard time saying "no." Others use them. Then, they "stuff" their anger. In other words, they put it in the back of their mind. Sometimes they say, "I never get angry." But the truth is, they just do not recognize it. They are scared of their feelings and do not want to face them. However, nothing gets accomplished. Problems do not get solved, so their anger, in fact, may grow.

Explosive (Aggressive) Anger: The opposite of passive is aggressive or explosive anger. People who have this characteristic tend to get angry very easily. They explode. They do not stop and ask questions or get more information. They are loud, antagonistic, and scary people. They often like to bully others and exercise much power and control. They often take advantage of passive people who are easily victimized. These people do not deal with their anger either. They just scream and yell, but they really are not working on their problems and may not even recognize why they are behaving the way they are.

Managing (Assertive) Anger: Managing anger is what you should aim for. Assertive people do just that. Assertive people do not victimize others. They are able to get their needs met by communicating, by problem-solving, and using anger-management tools. When you manage your anger, you recognize it for what it is, examine the options that you have to handle it, and then make a choice that is in the best interest of yourself and the people around you.

Exercise 6.3 Recognizing Your Anger

1. Check the characteristics that best fit you.

____ I am the quiet type. I let others do all the talking.

____ I believe that you "tell it like it is," no matter who gets hurt.

____ I just can't seem to say "no."

____ I am pretty good at communicating without stepping on other people's toes.

____ I have a short temper; sometimes, I just explode before I know what happened.

____ It seems like other people are always taking advantage of me, and it is hard for me to tell them what I'm really thinking.

____ People need to watch what they say to me because if they push my buttons, I just might go off on them.

____ I just keep my anger to myself; it is safer that way.

____ I let others know when they make me mad; no one has the right to look or say anything to me that is disrespectful.

____ I usually think about things before I act when I'm angry.

____ Generally, I think about how my actions are going to affect others before I act.

2. Examine the statements that you checked. Now, look back at the three categories of anger above. Which style most describes you? Discuss this with your group. You may find that other people see you differently than you see yourself.

_____
_____
_____
_____

Anger Cues and Triggers

To manage your anger, however, you must be able to recognize it. Now, we will review some of the ways to recognize anger and add a few more. They are not in any particular order.

- **Physical:** When angry, some people find that their breathing is fast and hard. They can feel their heart beating faster. Usually their shoulders and neck tighten up, and their fists clench. Sometimes they feel their head throbbing, their face may turn red. They may develop a stomachache or even throw up. What are your "anger symptoms?"

- **Thinking:** Often when people are angry, they are thinking "angry thoughts." For example, "She must be sleeping with someone else," "I'll get even, just wait." "No one gives a damn about me anyway." "He's not going to disrespect me like that." These angry thoughts can then lead to bad behavior.

- **Verbal:** Verbal cues have to do with words you might say out loud to yourself or others or, more frequently, what others say to you. For example, you know when you hear the words "lazy bastard," that you are going to react. Those two words have been known to "set you off" in the past. Until you examine why and make a choice not to let that happen again, it will continue to do so. However, if you say aloud to yourself, "What's the matter with me? I'm so stupid!" those are also verbal cues that could send you into an angry mood.

- **Environmental:** Our environment consists of all the scenery around us. That scenery has an emotional part to it. When we are in that scenery, we react the same way emotionally. For example, it could be the park where you meet your drug dealer and you anticipate getting high. It could be the bedroom where you and your partner argue about sex, money, or the children. It could be the shopping mall that sets you off due to bad purchasing choices in the past. Whatever your environmental cues are, you need to examine them and realize that today the situation is not the same as it was when this cue imprinted itself in your mind.

- **People:** People are often associated with environmental cues. In fact, they are a part of your environment. Some people may remind you of angry situations, past drug or alcohol use, or getting arrested. Not only do you need to recognize this as a cue that could set you off again, but you may need to avoid certain people or take them completely out of your life. This is especially true if they have been associated with substance abuse.

- **Situations:** Some situations may act as triggers. Think about bars (the environment and people present also, as well as verbal and thinking cues). How many fights have you gotten into as a result of the barroom scene, with peers or with your partner? Think about other situations. For example, think about being locked in prison where you can be accosted or threatened. Certainly, such situations can result in fear and anger. You are receiving a message that you must do something or the result could be bodily harm or death.

Anger Tools

Timeouts. One very valuable tool for stopping violence is a timeout. Timeouts work when one partner feels himself getting very angry, tense, or frustrated, and he says to his partner, "I'm beginning to feel angry, and I need to take a timeout." The person who calls for the timeout can leave the home for one hour—no longer, no shorter. This is a trust issue. Other rules for the timeout include:

- No cars, no bars while in timeout. In other words, no drinking, using, or driving. When you are angry, you do not think clearly. Therefore, if you go to the bar, you may end up angrier after a few drinks and some advice from other patrons.

- Do a physical activity, such as walking, running, bicycling, or gardening.

- Take a mental timeout also. Do not think about, dwell upon, or worry over the incident which just occurred. Return at the end of the hour and tell your partner you are back. Ask if she would like to talk about it now. If she says "no way," do not pursue it at this time. However, do not just forget it. Plan a time to discuss the incident and work on the issue.

- Use "I" language when talking with your partner (*see* Chapter 5: "Communication").

What if timeouts have not worked at your house? There may be several reasons. First, did you preplan the timeouts? Did you sit down and talk with your partner about it before you tried a timeout? Or, did you spring it on her suddenly when you were angry?

Did you work out a signal, something like referees use in football games? This signal can work very well, if you get too angry to talk. How about doing a few practice timeouts when you are not angry? If you do not do practice timeouts, you may never do a real one.

If your partner blocks the door or refuses to do a timeout with you, do not leave. You should try to go in the other room, possibly do a mental timeout, but do not force the situation.

If your partner has been drinking or using, do not try to do timeouts. While one might be needed, it is probably not safe at this time. Try to go to bed or gently and quietly remove yourself to a corner of the room. Do not argue with a person who is drinking or using. You cannot win and it may even be dangerous.

Healthy Communication. Perhaps one of the most valuable tools for dealing with anger is good communication. Open, honest, and direct expression of your feelings can provide the foundation for managing your anger. However, it is important to remember that this does not mean "letting it all hang out." What it does mean is taking into consideration the feelings and rights of the other people involved when you express your anger. Use nonoffensive language or body language.

Do not attack the other person. Sometimes you may get very frustrated when you feel the anger monster rising within you. However, if you attack the other person verbally, you will find that he gets defensive. Suddenly, you may find yourself involved in a power struggle. Remember, no one wins a power struggle! Avoid an attack. Instead, address the problem. What is the real issue? Stop the blame game. Take responsibility for your own feelings and behavior.

Focus on the current issue. What is the problem? Stay with it. Do not get off track and begin attacking the other person, as mentioned above. You might write the problem down, sit the paper down on the table in front of you, and then discuss it like adults. Also, avoid dragging in old issues.

Journal or write down your frustrations. This method of handling your anger is a time-proven one. It is one way of venting. It is also an excellent way of getting your brain to work. Now, you can start to see other ways of handling your emotions. You can see how you might have done things differently if you had taken some time to process your feelings.

Apologize now and then. There is nothing wrong with saying, "I'm sorry" once in a while. Sometimes, it is okay to say "I'm sorry" when the situation was not your fault. It happens in business all the time when a clerk, for example, apologizes to a customer when the customer was at fault.

Admit when you are wrong. Go ahead. It won't kill you. You might have to swallow a little bit of pride, but why not? People will often respect you more when you have the courage to say, "I blew it."

Use visualization. In visualization, you picture yourself in a beautiful, peaceful place, perhaps a spot you remember from your childhood. Then, you use all your senses—you smell the air, you see the beautiful stream and trees, you taste the moisture in the air, you feel the water in the stream. In other words, you try to make this image very real in your mind. Once you have created this place, it is yours—no one else's. You can go there anytime that you feel angry and stressed. You can go there instantly and in only a few mini-seconds, you can feel the anger pass.

Examine other stress busters. Later in this chapter, you will find the section on stress. Stress and anger go hand-in-hand. You can use many of the same tools to combat anger that you use to combat stress. This includes things like developing recreational activities, or engaging in meditation and prayers, or asking for help. Read that section carefully. Use as many tools as you need to assist you with anger management.

> **Remember! There is no decision you can make when you are angry that you cannot make better when you are not angry.**

"Early Florida" by JG. Media: Acrylic paint on canvas and custom-made wood frame. Courtesy of Art Behind Bars.

Exercise 6.4 Types of Anger

1. List the types of anger you have used and describe them in detail.

_____
_____
_____
_____
_____
_____
_____
_____

2. Describe your anger cues or triggers.

_____
_____
_____
_____
_____
_____
_____
_____

Fill in the following anger journal each week during the rest of your program. It is okay to make copies of this form. Share your completed entry with your counselor, instructor, or another person with whom you feel safe and comfortable sharing.

Exercise 6.5 Anger Journal (Note: You can copy this page)

Date and time of incident: _____

What was the incident that triggered the situation?

_____
_____
_____
_____

What were your body signs or cues?

_____
_____
_____
_____

What was your response? How did you handle it?

_____
_____
_____
_____

Did you stuff your feelings? _____ Escalate it? _____ Or, did you manage it? _____

List what you can do in the future to better manage your anger?

_____
_____
_____
_____

Stress Contributors

As mentioned earlier, stress and anger are closely related. When you are stressed, anger can and often does result. If you do not do something to relieve the stress, it can lead to more anger and more stress. The results can be physically and emotionally harmful. Therefore, it is important to develop skills for recognizing stress and to combat it before it gets out of control.

Situations: As with anger, situations often produce stress. Examples of situations could be a partner cheating on you, a boss who never listens, being locked in jail, losing a job, or learning you are HIV-positive. Stress also can develop from situations which are not as serious, but from lesser frustrations that continue over a period of time. For example, your children continue to stay out late in spite of your insisting they come in before curfew; you lock your keys in the car and have to pay to get them out; you lose $40 out of your pocket in the mall; you get a flat tire on the way to work. Over time, a series of events can lead to intense stress, so much so that a person suffers medical and mental health problems.

Good and bad things happen to people. Sometimes it may seem like only the bad things happen to you. But, in reality, if you look back, you probably could find a number of good things as well. An inmate once said, "I'm really glad I'm locked up here." Most inmates do not say that. Most are angry and bitter about their sentences and leaving their family and lifestyle on the street. When asked why, he replied, "I'd be dead if I was on the street."

Negative Management: Many people deal with stress by trying to run from it, hide it, or cover it up. They can do this in a variety of ways. The following is a list, but it is not complete. You can probably add your own method of coping with stress.

- Using alcohol or drugs
- Spending money you do not have to spare
- Blaming others for your problems
- Driving fast and recklessly
- Chain smoking
- Feeling sorry for yourself
- Isolating yourself
- Sleeping too much

- Thinking about suicide
- Overeating or not eating

Positive Management: If you have been using negative ways to manage stress, perhaps it is time to change your way of thinking. What else can you do to change your attitude and the outcome? Granted, if you are locked up, some of the methods may not work at this time, but you can keep them in mind for when you are free. Again, you can probably find other ways to help you manage stress, ways that are not on this list.

- Write in a journal
- Exercise, walk, jog, run, or work out
- Practice meditating or deep breathing
- Use your faith actively, pray, talk to a spiritual adviser
- Listen to music
- Read a book
- Watch TV
- Practice and expand your hobbies—develop hobbies if you do not have them now
- Take a timeout to think about your options
- Ask for help from a trusted friend or a counselor
- Redirect your thinking and activities

In life, we always will have stress—good stress and bad stress. Stress means we are alive.

Exercise 6.6 Stress Management

List negative and positive ways you have managed stress in the past or currently.

Negative	Positive
_____	_____
_____	_____
_____	_____
_____	_____
_____	_____
_____	_____
_____	_____
_____	_____

"Man with Mask" by BP. Media: Shoe polish, ink, coffee creamer, brown bag, zine cutouts, food coloring, and pencil on recycled cardboard. Courtesy of Art Behind Bars.

Chapter 7:
The Role of Substance Abuse
(3–4 Sessions)

Objectives

▶ To understand the role substance abuse plays in domestic violence

▶ To examine how substance abuse affects family systems

▶ To develop healthy methods of coping with life stressors

▶ To examine your own history of substance abuse and violence

Basic Concepts of Substance Abuse

Definition of a Drug: A drug is a substance that changes or alters the way a person feels, thinks, or acts. This simple and basic definition often is used in treatment programs. Whether you are thinking about an aspirin or cocaine, the same statement applies. However, there is a big difference between taking an aspirin for a headache and injecting cocaine to get high. We will discuss various types of substances.

Types of Drugs

Depressants: Depressants are drugs that depress the central nervous system. They are sometimes called "downers" because they slow down the nervous system or suppress it. Some of these drugs include alcohol, barbiturates, tranquilizers, and heroin.

Stimulants: Stimulants are the opposite of depressants. They are also known as "uppers" because they speed up or excite the nervous system. Some of these drugs include cocaine, methamphetamine, amphetamines, and caffeine.

Marijuana: Marijuana is often classified by itself today, although you will see it listed as a mental stimulant at times and as a downer at other times. This occurs because marijuana has many different properties. There are many different types of marijuana, which can produce different effects. In addition, marijuana is often laced with other drugs, so a person may not know what he really has taken.

Hallucinogens: These include LSD, PCP, Ecstasy, and mushrooms. These drugs are not considered to be physically addictive, but they are mentally addictive. In other words, the person likes the feelings he or she gets from their use and continues to use to get that high.

Prescription drugs: Many people become addicted to prescription drugs. Sometimes a person may get a prescription for pain following surgery, and he gets "hooked" on that drug. He likes the feeling, so he may lie about his pain to get another prescription or go to a different doctor or even steal to obtain the drug. Examples of these painkillers include Vicodin, Percocet, and Oxycontin.

Over-the-counter (OTC) drugs: Some people think because they can go in the store and buy legal drugs over the counter that they are not dangerous. This is far from the truth. Overuse and long-term use of any drug can be dangerous. Especially dangerous is mixing over-the-counter drugs or prescription drugs with alcohol and/or other drugs. This mixture can be deadly. Never, never drink or use drugs if you are on other medications. This includes sinus, allergy, and aspirin medications.

Withdrawal and effects on brain chemistry: Withdrawal or indirect effects of drugs on the human body are usually the opposite of the direct effect. Think about what happens when you take cocaine. You get high, right? Your brain neurotransmitters are jumping up and down and all over the place. What happens when you quit taking the cocaine? You can go into a cocaine depression, the body slows down, you feel slow, tired and indifferent. The brain is actually crying "MORE, MORE, FEED ME," because it is suffering from withdrawal.

The same thing occurs with alcohol. Since it is a depressant, when you drink, the alcohol depresses the central nervous system. Watch people who are drunk. They may have slowed or slurred speech, their motor coordination decreases, their judgment goes. They may get aggressive or drowsy. What happens when they quit drinking? They start shaking, get agitated and irritable, get scared, or have much anxiety. Again, the brain is crying "MORE, MORE, FEED ME." That is why a person reaches for a drink the first thing in the morning after a night out. Eventually, a person may even have "DTs," a withdrawal process where the person hallucinates, maybe even thinks bugs are crawling all over his body.

Use, abuse, and dependency: Most people can attend a social event and have a beer and suffer no after effects. They have a drink or two, but they do not have five or six. They do not abuse the alcohol. They do not become addicted. Remember, there is a difference between use, abuse, and dependency. Some people can drink occasionally and moderately with no problem. However, some people cannot. The alcoholic cannot. One drink generally will start the alcoholic on a relapse cycle. It will set up a craving within him. You may have heard an alcoholic say "I can't have just one." He knows from his personal history what can happen with that one drink.

Abuse may or may not lead to dependency. But it is just what the name says. It is drinking too much, getting drunk or high. It produces problems with judgment and memory. It can be costly—not only costing you money, but contributing to violence, abuse, and loss of relationships.

Dependency goes a step further. It, too, may include abuse and usually does. However, dependency occurs when a person becomes physically and mentally addicted. His body craves the alcohol; his brain remembers how it felt—the high or the mellowing out, the forgetting of problems (although temporarily), the seeming increase of self-esteem, the fun that he had with friends when drinking. All of these memories work together with the withdrawal (physical craving) to make him want to keep using and, therefore, keeps him a prisoner to addiction.

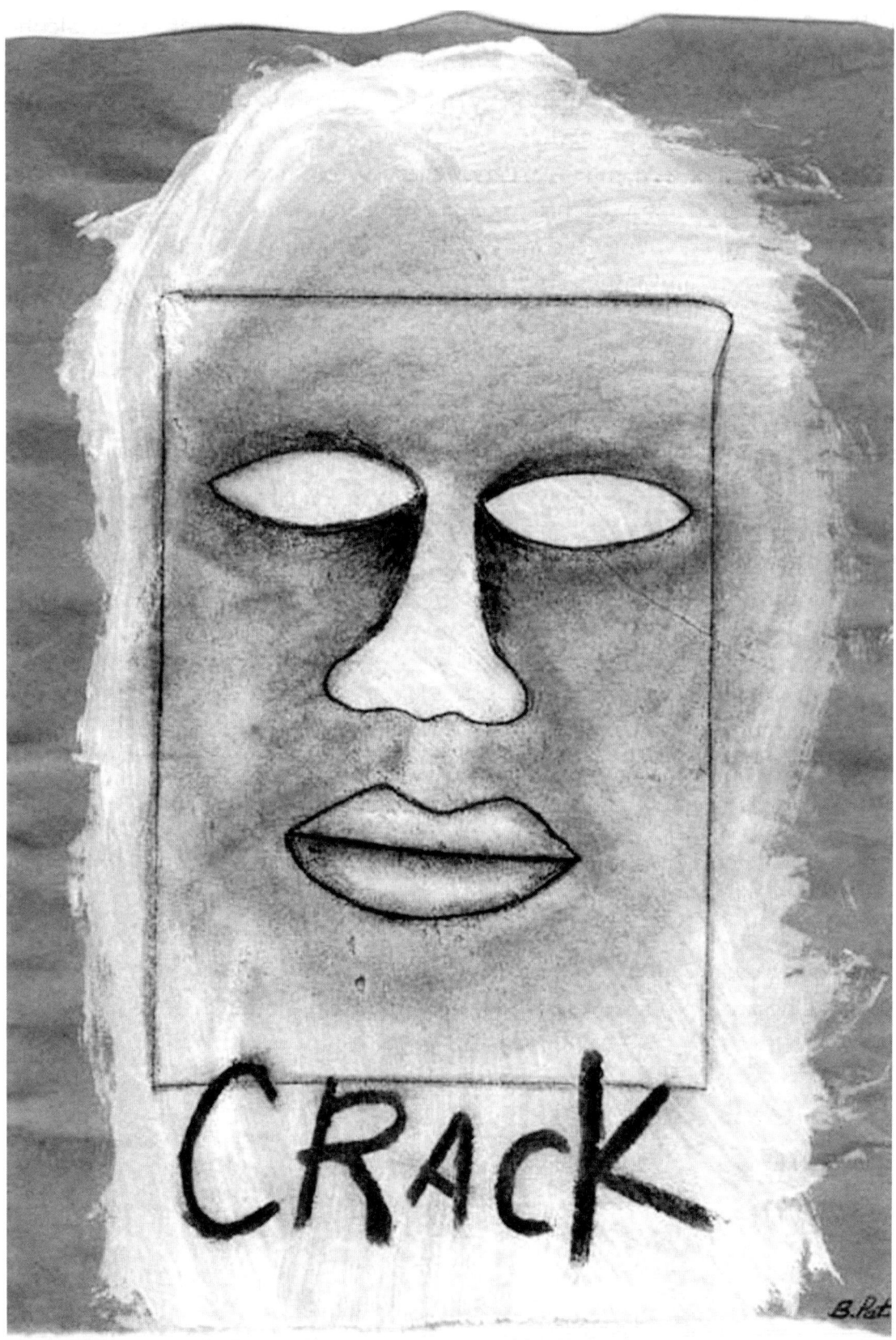

"Crack" by BP. Media: Toothpaste, pen, pink highlighter, black marker on brown paper bag. Courtesy of Art Behind Bars.

Exercise 7.1 Types of Drugs

1. Put the following drugs in their correct category. Put a D for Depressant, S for Stimulant, H for Hallucinogen, OTC for Over-the-Counter, and P for Prescription.

____ Heroin	____ Cocaine	____ Marijuana
____ Benadryl	____ Percocet	____ LSD
____ Methamphetamine	____ Mushrooms	____ Vicodin
____ Ecstasy	____ Caffeine	____ Alcohol
____ Barbiturates	____ Prozac	____ Tobacco

2. Describe your past or current substance use and the outcomes.

_____

_____

_____

_____

_____

Effects of Drugs on Domestic Violence

Inability to manage feelings or communicate needs: Many people use alcohol and other substances to manage their feelings. Perhaps you are one of these people. Perhaps you never felt comfortable with your feelings, whether they were good or bad feelings. Bad feelings can be scary, making us want to run away from them. But good feelings also can be frightening. They may feel like "this isn't going to last. It will all go away soon, and I'll be right back where I was." So, you may have spent a lot of time running from your feelings, hiding them, pretending that they did not exist. And, of course, one way to do this is to drink or use other substances.

In a relationship, people who are drinking or using may hurt the ones they love. They may say things they do not mean, become irritable, lash out, even strike out. In addition, long-term abuse can contribute to paranoia and even aggression. It also can lead to poor decision making.

Stress, anger/domestic violence connection: This connection was discussed in depth in Chapter 7: "Anger, Stress, and Domestic Violence." You may want to review that information here. However, the important thing to remember is that drinking or using does not usually (with a few exceptions, such as PCP) cause violence. The word "cause" is a scientific term, which means that every time someone drinks or uses they get aggressive and beat someone up. This does not happen. Some people who beat others up never drink or use drugs. However, there is a strong connection. An estimated 75 to 85 percent of men involved in domestic violence episodes were drinking or using at the time of the incident.

Finances: Did you ever spend too much money at the bar? Did you ever have your wife or partner yell at you because there was not enough money for the bills because you spent it at the liquor store or bar? Think about the cost of drinking or using. But do not just add up the cost of the liquor or drug. Add the cost of your bail money, your court fines, your attorney, the additional car insurance, and any reimbursement to victims. And, do not forget the cost of doing treatment or classes. The final number may astound you. In fact, you may have been able to buy a new car or at least make a good down payment on a home with that money!

Family activities: One of the areas that suffer when a family member does alcohol or other drugs is family activities. Usually the person is focused on the substance; it comes first. So he may spend a lot of time with his contacts, making drug deals, using the drug, getting high. And, then, he withdraws, becomes irritable, and is difficult to live with. His whole world is centered on his drug. Anyone who gets in the way is easily shoved aside.

Loss of control/judgment: This was mentioned earlier, but think back to your own activities. Did you ever have a moment when you lost control? Are there any times when you made decisions that were not in your best interest? Did you ever do something really stupid under the influence, which you regretted later? Many, many inmates say "yes" to those questions. A large number of them admit they would not be where they are (imprisoned or on parole) if they had not made a poor decision to drink and drive or to use drugs and rob someone for money, possessions, or drugs.

Family roles assumed: In a family system, people assume roles to help them survive. Because the use of alcohol and other drugs is often a part of domestic violence, family members may be taking on specific roles to cope with both the substance abuse and the domestic abuse. If you have ever taken drug and alcohol classes, you probably have heard these roles discussed. Sharon Wegscheider, a psychologist, has developed a theory based on a family system's model; she describes the following roles:

- **Dependent Person:** This is the person who is dependent on the alcohol or other substance. This person is obsessed with alcohol or drugs and his behavior is often aggressive, angry, blaming, self-righteous, abusive, critical, and unpredictable. What he really feels inside is a sense of self-hatred, guilt, helplessness, hurt, and rejection. He often is using a substance to cope with problems instead of handling them.

- **The Enabler (sometimes known as the co-dependent):** Usually this is the spouse. This person helps or "enables" the dependent to remain in his condition by making excuses to others for his "illness," by completing tasks he cannot do while withdrawing from the substance, or by financially bailing out the family when the dependent cannot hold a job. The enabler spends a lot of time trying to protect the dependent from consequences. Generally, this person means well, but acts out of a misguided sense of love and loyalty. She [or he] often feels angry and powerless, has poor self-esteem, and feels like a failure. Often, she does not see any options to her situation.

- **Family Hero:** Usually this is the oldest child, who seems successful at everything he or she tries. This child may take on the role of parent, even parenting his parents. These children are often very helpful to the family and successful outside the home. They have a façade of being happy and good-natured and are generally high-performing individuals. However, they are subject to extreme stress and their own needs are rarely satisfied. They have a poor self-image.

- **Scapegoat:** This person gets in trouble a lot—at home and at school. Generally, he gets the blame when things go wrong. These children crave attention. When they do not get it by being good, they often behave negatively. They often withdraw from the family and rely on the peer group, often turning to alcohol or other drugs. They assume a reverse role of the Family Hero.

- **Lost Child:** Usually this is a quiet and shy person who is easy to get along with. This individual appears to sense tension in the family, feels confused, and adapts by getting lost. The family is often too preoccupied to notice this child's needs and because he withdraws, they often do not see a problem with this child. Often this child lives in his or her own fantasy world. This child has very low self-expectations.

- **Mascot:** Like clowns, these people are always kidding around and joking. They are hyperactive, usually attracting much attention. This child is often the youngest and is protected and babied. They know there is a problem in the family and become frightened and confused. They cope with these feelings by creating fun, and showing off a lot. They also may demonstrate erratic behavior or annoying habits. They may act cute or helpless.

Remember, all of these individuals may feel confused, helpless, and hurt inside. They are struggling to cope with problems but may not have adequate tools. As a result, they have taken on these roles. Remember also that when the domestic violence is complicated by substance use, it becomes even more difficult for family members to cope.

While these are only brief descriptions, you may be able to see a pattern where you and other members of your family fit. Each of these family members may feel hurt, pain, loneliness, and often are very confused. They may feel inadequate, insecure, angry, and afraid. Playing their role is their way of dealing with their feelings in the substance-dependent household.

Exercise 7.2 Effects of Substance Use on Family Violence

1. Review the list of the effects of substance use on family violence. Do you recall any of these affecting your family life? If so, which ones? Describe the effect.

_____
_____
_____
_____

2. Did anyone in your family have a problem with drugs or alcohol? Who was it (no name needed), what substance was used, and how do you think that affected you?

_____
_____
_____
_____
_____
_____
_____

3. Refer back to the list of "Family roles assumed." Can you identify any role you may have taken on as a child? If so, describe which one. Name other family members who took on roles as well. Discuss with your group why you may have taken on this role.

_____

_____

_____

_____

Other Factors of Substance Use/Abuse

Because alcohol and other substance use or abuse affects your judgment, it also may result in you making poor choices. Such decisions can have a significant impact on your life and the lives of others. For example, look at the following areas:

HIV/AIDS, hepatitis, and sexually transmitted diseases (STDs): One of the primary ways in which the HIV virus is spread is through sexual contact. Have you ever had unprotected sex when under the influence or drunk? Think about a few moments of "fun" or "pleasure" and how those moments could result in your death—or be spread to others you love. Consider also other transmitted diseases through needle use, such as hepatitis and STDs.

Legal implications: These include driving under the influence (DUI), tickets, the alcohol/drug classes and treatment, the loss of money, time, and other problems. For some, this may have gone even further. You may be here because you injured or killed a person while under the influence of alcohol or another substance. Not only do you have to deal with the legal implications, but you have to deal with the emotional trauma, the guilt, and the knowledge of what you did for the rest of your life.

Unwanted relationships and pregnancies: As mentioned earlier, the results of unprotected sex can be diseases. However, another "side effect" is that people get themselves in positions where they feel "trapped." Often, this can be the result of an unplanned pregnancy in which the man feels duty-bound to the relationship. He may not even love the woman, but now a child is on the way. Therefore, he remains with her, may even marry her, but is a reluctant groom. This can lead to resentment and hostilities, resulting in domestic violence. Or, he may feel hostile about being required to pay child support.

Exercise 7.3 Substance Abuse in Your Life

A. Describe how substance abuse affected these areas in your life: (1) health, (2) sex, (3) legal problems.

_____
_____
_____
_____
_____

B. What are your future plans for the use of alcohol and/or drugs in your life? How do you see your past use at this time?

_____
_____
_____
_____
_____

Chapter 8: Problem Solving and Conflict Management

(2–3 Sessions)

Objectives

▶ To develop positive conflict-resolution skills

▶ To identify and use a problem-solving model

▶ To examine options of decision making

▶ To translate knowledge into personal skills

Problem Solving and Domestic Violence

What do you do when you have a problem? How do you solve it? Do you even think about it? Or, do you just react? People may do several different things when faced with a problem. They may pretend the problem does not exist and hide from it, or they may make a decision without thinking about it (react). Such quick decisions are based on our feelings of the moment. When we do not take time and consider the outcome or consequences of our decisions, the results can be disastrous.

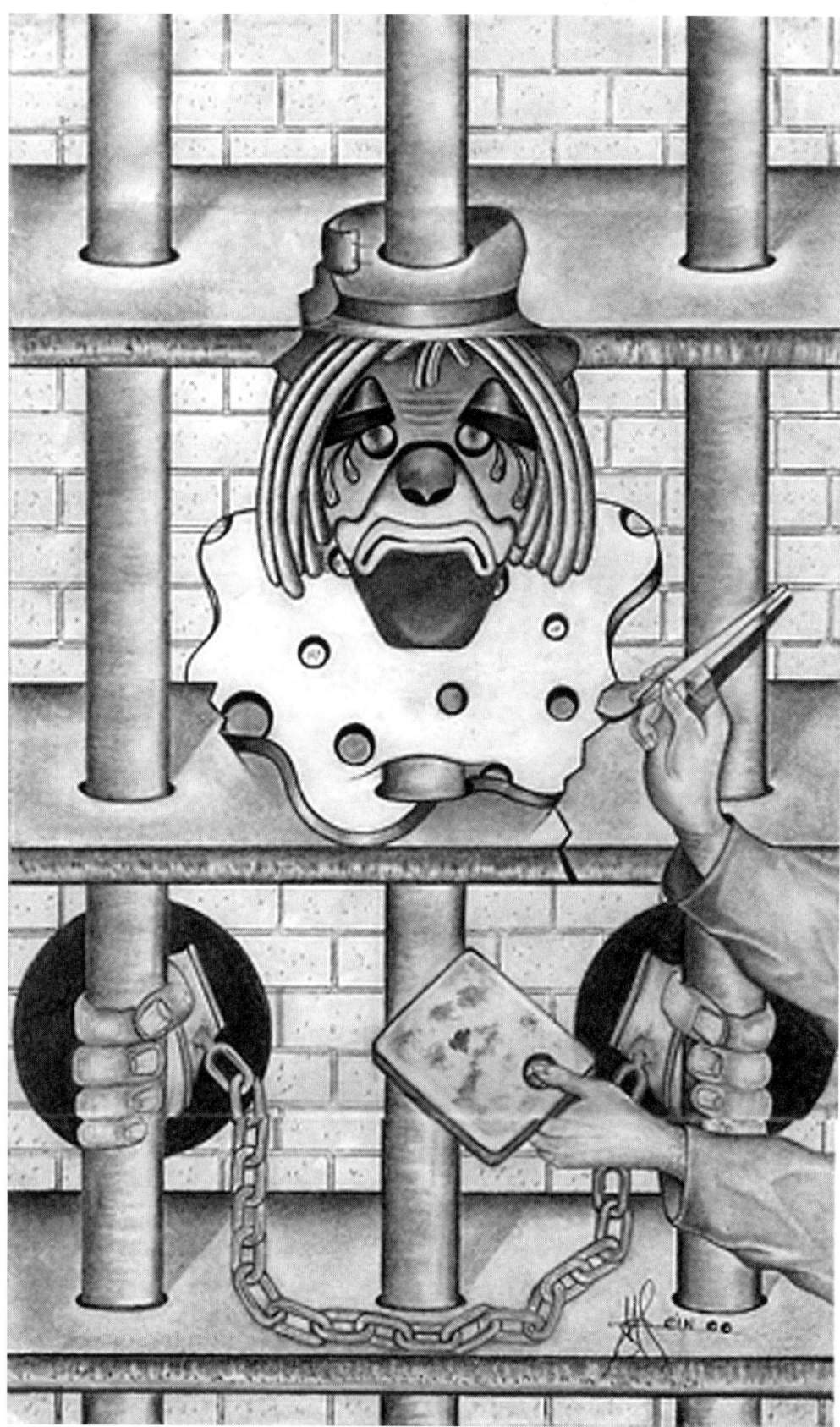

"Clown Behind Bars" by MS. Media: Pencil on legal paper. Courtesy of Art Behind Bars.

It is very important for you to consider your partner's needs and concerns when problem solving. When this does not happen, your partner may be angry, frustrated, or resentful. Tempers may flare. You may find yourself arguing over petty things and the tension will increase. You may not realize why the other person is upset. The key point here is that you must include all parties who are involved in the decision-making process.

The following model may help you in handling relationship problems, as well as problems in many other areas.

Problem-Solving Model

1. **STOP.** Slow down and listen. What is being said? It is almost impossible to make a good decision when you are agitated. So, relax. Give yourself a few minutes to consider the situation.

2. **WHAT IS THE PROBLEM?** This may seem like a foolish question, but the truth is that often you may not know the real problem. People who go for marriage counseling may say the problem is communication, but that may only be the symptom of the real problem. Get very specific and narrow down the problem.

3. **GATHER ADDITIONAL INFORMATION NEEDED.** Perhaps you do not have enough information to solve the problem. Maybe you need more facts, such as costs, deadlines, knowledge of who will be affected, and so forth. Where can you get the information?

4. **LIST ALL POSSIBLE SOLUTIONS**. This step is also known as *brainstorming*. List solutions that may sound impossible or silly. At this stage, list everything. This step just helps you to explore and seek all possible answers to the problem.

5. **ELIMINATE IMPOSSIBLE SOLUTIONS**. Go back and look at all solutions. Which ones are impossible or silly? Cross those out.

6. **SELECT TWO-TO-THREE POSSIBLE SOLUTIONS**. Now, talk about the pros and cons of each solution. Everyone involved should contribute to this process. Keep a second plan or Plan B as a backup--just in case Plan A does not work.

7. **NARROW DOWN TO ONE SOLUTION**. Make sure this solution is acceptable to all. This does not mean that everyone has to agree on all the fine points, but it does mean they can "live with it." In other words, they are willing to try.

8. **PUT THE SOLUTION INTO ACTION**. "Do it." Try it. See what happens.

9. **REVIEW and EVALUATE THE SOLUTION**. Is it working? What parts are working? Which parts are not working? If the problem is not being resolved, you may need to:

10. **MODIFY THE SOLUTION**. Discuss this with everyone involved. Again, get all opinions and then implement the modification. Then, evaluate again. If the solution is still not working:

11. **GO TO PLAN B**. Remember in Step 6, when you were instructed to keep a second plan on hold just in case Plan A did not work? Now, follow Steps 7 through 10 to implement plan B. Evaluate it and modify it, if necessary.

You can improve your problem solving by understanding how important the thought process is. Everyone interprets events differently. When you recognize that your partner may not see the world as you do, you can ask questions, learn what her ideas, attitudes, and beliefs are about the world, and how that may affect her perceptions. You also can modify your interpretation of events.

In addition, you always can be a fact-finder. Often our reactions to events surrounding us are emotional, without facts. Look for the facts. Seek evidence before making a decision or reacting in a way that might prove disastrous. For example, a man heard that his wife was having an affair. He went home and confronted her about the gossip. During the argument, he pulled a gun on her. She reported this action. He was arrested for domestic violence. Because he was a police officer under the laws of his state, he will never work in law enforcement again.

Be sure you have the facts!

Exercise 8.1 Problem Resolution

Select a problem from the past or a current one either with a partner or someone living closely with you. Using the model above, outline how you could have solved the problem or will solve the problem in the future.

1. Stop. Slow down and listen. Think about the situation. Write your thoughts.

_____

_____

2. What is the real problem? Make sure this is specific.

_____

_____

3. What information do I need to help me solve the problem? Where can I get it?

_____

_____

_____

4. Now, list all possible solutions (brainstorm).

_____

_____

_____

_____

5. Eliminate or get rid of impossible solutions. Go back over them and cross them out.

_____

_____

6. Select two-to-three possible solutions. Write down the pros and cons of each.

_____

_____

_____

_____

_____

7. Narrow your choice down to one solution that everyone can live with.
_____
_____

8. Put the solution into action. Try it. See if it works. (If you are not yet in a position to do this, imagine the outcome).
_____
_____

9. If you are in a position to do this, review and evaluate the solution. Is it working?
_____
_____

10. If the solution is not working, modify or alter it a bit.
_____
_____

11. If you are in position to do this and if it is needed, go to Plan B. You may not be able to do the last three-to-four steps at this time. But you can imagine the outcome and you can use this model whenever you are seeking a method to help you problem solve.

Conflict Management

The inability to manage conflict is probably one of the biggest hurdles in relationships. People who cannot manage conflict end up arguing and fighting much of the time. They cannot effectively solve problems. Problem solving and conflict management work together. People who cannot manage conflict usually cannot solve problems successfully. We will examine both nonproductive and productive ways to manage conflict.

Nonproductive Conflict Management

- **Avoidance:** Do you like conflict? Most people do not, so what they do is run from it and try to avoid it. They may leave the scene, fall asleep, or turn up the stereo to avoid talking with the other person. But sometimes people avoid conflict emotionally by refusing to deal with the problem. At other times, they refuse to discuss it or to listen to the other person's side of the story. Sometimes, they just hammer away at the other person, until that person gives in. Notice that the conflict is never dealt with. It is just avoided. In other words, they do not reach a solution.

- **Force:** When confronted with conflict, some people try to force their way of thinking on the other person by using physical or emotional force. The person who "wins" is the one who exerts the most force. Still, issues are avoided.

- **Minimization:** This occurs when you make light of the situation. You may say and perhaps believe that the conflict is not really important. You may make light of the other person's feelings.

- **Blame:** One way that people fail to deal with the situation is by blaming someone else for the conflict. Sometimes a person blames himself, but more often, he blames someone else. This temporarily relieves some guilt.

- **Silencing:** Another way some people deal with the situation is by silencing the other person. One way to do this is by crying. Another way is to yell, scream, or pretend to lose control. Another is to get sick, experience headaches, shortness of breath, or other symptoms. One problem is that your partner may not be sure if this is a tactic to win the argument or if it is a real physical problem.

- **Gunnysacking:** Do you know what a gunnysack is? Picture a large burlap bag. In gunnysacking, a person stores up his complaints and then unloads them on the other person when an argument occurs. Even after unloading his grievances, he puts them all back in the sack so he can dump them out again at a later date.

- **Manipulation:** In manipulation, people try to avoid open conflict. They may divert attention by acting charming, with the idea of getting the other person into a receptive and noncombative mood before disagreement. The situation is manipulated so that the person doing the manipulation eventually wins the battle, argument, or disagreement.

- **Personal rejection:** Nothing is more frustrating than when a person withholds love and seeks to win an argument by getting the other person to break down as a result. Have you ever acted cold or uncaring, refusing to hug or kiss because you were angry? Once the other person feels rejected, it may be easier for you to get your way. This is another form of manipulation. You are making your love contingent upon getting your way.

Productive Conflict Resolution

- **Fight above the belt:** Refuse to fight dirty. If you wound your partner's spirit, it may be very difficult for that person to recover. Avoid causing hostility and resentment.

- **Fight actively:** This does not mean physically fighting with your partner. What it means is to stay open minded and to participate in the discussion. If conflicts are to be resolved, both parties need to actively participate in the process.

- **Take responsibility for your part:** Resist avoiding responsibility by putting the blame on your partner or someone or something else. Own your own thoughts and feelings. Use "I" messages.

- **Be direct and specific:** Focus on the here-and-now. Avoid situations or feelings that occurred in the past. Stick to the issue and focus on observable behaviors. Avoid mind reading.

- **Use humor for relief, never for ridicule:** Humor is awesome. It is healing. However, people sometimes use it in a sarcastic manner to embarrass the other person. Such use of humor can make the conflict worse. Use it in a healthy manner, to provide a break in the tension. Do not use it as a manipulative device to win the battle or put down the other person. Also, it is important to know your partner and how she will take the humor.

Remember: honor and respect. This should be at the heart of your relationships with others. If you keep this in mind, then you should be better able to avoid negative ways of dealing with conflict and approach the situation with tenderness and concern.

Exercise 8.2 Nonproductive and Productive Conflict Resolution

List three ways that you have used nonproductive conflict resolution in the past. Then, review them and write the ways you could have handled the conflict in a productive manner.

Nonproductive Conflict Resolution:

1. _____
   _____
   _____

2. _____
   _____
   _____

3. _____
   _____
   _____

Productive Conflict Resolution:

1. _____
   _____
   _____

2. _____
   _____
   _____

3. _____
   _____
   _____

"Self-Portrait on 3/26/05" by BP. Media: Mustard, grape Kool-Aid™ powder, marker, and crayon on recycled corrugated cardboard box. Courtesy of Art Behind Bars.

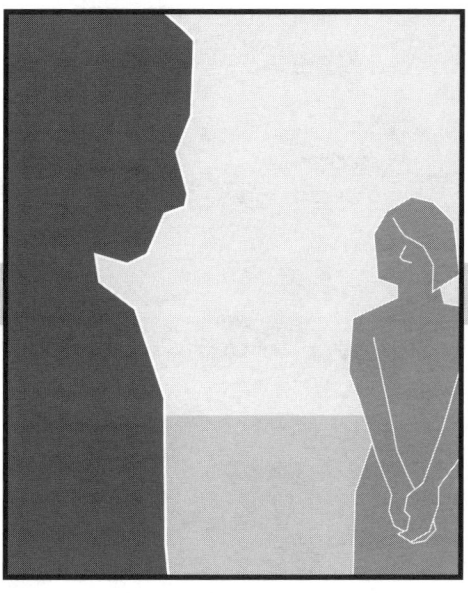

Chapter 9: Self-Management
(4–5 Sessions)

Objectives

▶ To define relapse prevention as it pertains to domestic violence

▶ To further examine consequences of behavior

▶ To explore personal moral codes and values and build on them

▶ To develop a personal-prevention plan

Carrying "Old Baggage"

"Old baggage" refers to holding on to past wounds and refusing to forgive the other person. It refers to throwing up the past to the other person when a new argument arises. "Old baggage" stops us from thinking clearly and adds to our inability to say "no" to behavior that may not be in our best interest. It also generates distorted thinking ideas and patterns.

Some examples of "old baggage" include:

- Hatred
- Grudges

- Anger
- Jealousy
- Revenge
- Unresolved grief
- Sense of neglect
- Sense of abandonment
- Spite
- Past mistakes
- Irresponsibility
- Sense of inadequacy or imperfection
- Lack of accomplishment

"Old baggage" can be internal or external. It can reflect the way we feel toward others or toward ourselves. It is like a cancer. It grows out of control, overtaking the healthy cells around it and destroying them. It can produce sickness, both physical and emotional. Eventually, it can produce physical and emotional death.

The results of carrying "old baggage" around can be the following:

- Stress/anger
- Illness
- Vengeful thinking/plans
- Inability or unwillingness to change
- Criminal activity
- Substance abuse
- Bad or lost relationships
- Loss of time and/or money
- Loss of productive energy

Most of us have "old baggage" hanging around. It comes from experiences we have had on our journey through life. Often, we do not recognize it because it wears many masks. But it is up to you to be a detective and spot signs of old baggage.

Exercise 9.1 Old Baggage Checklist

Use the following checklist to help you determine if you are carrying around old baggage.

_____ 1. You tend to carry grudges, anger, and resentment around old situations.

_____ 2. You feel like you are justified in carrying such hostilities.

_____ 3. It feels good to "hit people over the head" with this old information.

_____ 4. You have a hard time forgiving people for past perceived wrongs.

_____ 5. You get a "benefit" from carrying this feeling around.

_____ 6. You turn to substance use when you dwell on past hurts.

_____ 7. You blame others for the outcome of past perceived hurts.

If you checked several of these items, look more closely at your use of old baggage. First of all, examine specific situations that generated the feelings. Then, look at the cost of carrying the "old baggage." Is it hurting your relationships with others? Is it worth impacting your life? In the "big picture" of life, is this a mountain or a molehill? Is forgiveness possible at this time? If not, can you let go of the power of the event, so that it is not controlling you and your behavior? Visualize the situation with a different outcome. Continue to take inventory and practice change. Be honest with yourself.

Finally when "old baggage" rears its head again, and it will, continue to remove it from your thoughts and replace those thoughts with something more positive. If possible, make amends with the person involved in the situation. If not possible, make amends within yourself.

Self-Talk

Self-talk can be constructive or destructive. In other words, it can be a powerful friend, to help you to get through tough times or it can cause you to grumble and groan about all the terrible things that have happened to you but you never get any wiser.

What does self-talk mean? It refers to the messages that you give yourself. For example, have you ever said, "I'm so stupid. Why do I keep doing the same dumb things over and over?" Or "I was born on the wrong side of the tracks. I just never had the luck that other people have." These kinds of statements can defeat you.

The story is told about the man who was being paroled to California. His cellmate had once lived in California. One day he asked him, "What kind of people live in California?" The cellmate thought a moment and answered, "What kind of people lived where you came from?" The man didn't hesitate. He spoke up with an angry tone in his voice. "They were stupid, dumb, just looking after themselves. Taking advantage of everyone who got in their way, mean-spirited, greedy people!" He paused a second. "Why?" "Well, I'm afraid you will find those same kind of people in California."

You take you with you, wherever you go. So, if you are thinking negatively, if you believe the world is mean and cruel, then you will indeed find people like that. Your self-talk, coupled with your beliefs, can create your surroundings.

Remember, negative beliefs rule much of our lives. It is extremely important as you move toward developing a healthier, balanced lifestyle, that you get rid of this negative self-talk. Instead, focus on positive self-talk.

Positive self-talk includes statements that work against the negative ideas. For example, if you catch yourself saying "I'm so stupid," immediately change it. "I do some things right, some things very well." Remind yourself of the activities you have done correctly. Pat yourself on the back once in a while. In spite of the mistakes you have made in your life, you have done some good things also. In other words, you have personal strengths.

Use affirmations. Affirmations are strong, positive statements saying that something you want is already true. It requires practice to do this. An example of this is "I have a very good job."(Say this even when you may not feel that way at the moment). Or "I will wake up at 6 a.m. and feel rested in the morning." Usually the shorter and simpler the affirmation, the more effective it will be.

Your affirmations should be expressed in your own words. When you do affirmations, you are not trying to redo or change what already exists. You are simply creating something new—a new outlook, a new way of acting that will be in your best interest. You need to put your full belief into the affirmation. However, affirmations are not meant to change your feelings. If you are sad, you cannot and should not affirm that you are happy.

Creative visualization is another way to help combat negative self-talk. Use your imagination to focus on what you would like to happen in your life. This technique can be used with affirmations to help you create a clear image of something you wish to happen. For example, think of something you would like to happen or obtain. Count to ten slowly and relax your body. Now, imagine yourself having or doing the thing you want. Make some positive affirmations while doing this. Use all your senses when you visualize (sight, smell, hearing, touch, and taste). If negative thoughts intrude, refocus on the visualization.

Another way to use visualization is when you are stressed or angry. You calm your body and imagine yourself in a very peaceful place. It might be a scene from your childhood, such as a mountain scene with a lake. Or, it could be a room. You create this place in your head. Then, you use all your senses to experience it. You smell the flowers, taste the moisture in the air, and feel the wind on your face. In other words, the more of your senses you use, the more real the scene is and the more it will help you to relax. Once you have this place of your very own, you can go there very quickly, instantly, when negative thoughts or stressors come into your life. It provides you with a very quick way to relax and ease the tension.

Exercise 9.2 Your Personal Strengths

Stop and consider your personal strengths for a while. What do you do well or at least okay? Examine the following areas: family, work, spiritual beliefs, hobbies, skills, and values.

A. Now, list at least three of your specific strengths.

1. _____

2. _____

3. _____

B. What are some ways that you can build on these strengths?

_____

_____

_____

_____

Personal Care and Balance

Balance is a very important part of a healthy relationship. As human beings, we need balance to keep us emotionally and physically healthy. Eastern philosophies talk about Yin and Yang, male and female, and other dualities. The idea is that whenever we fail to maintain any area of our lives, we will throw ourselves out of balance. For example, if you neglect the physical area, you may end up sick. This also can affect all the other areas. You cannot do your work well if you are sick. You also cannot interact as well with your family and friends. Certainly, your emotional state will be affected.

Review the sections of the Balance Wheel below.

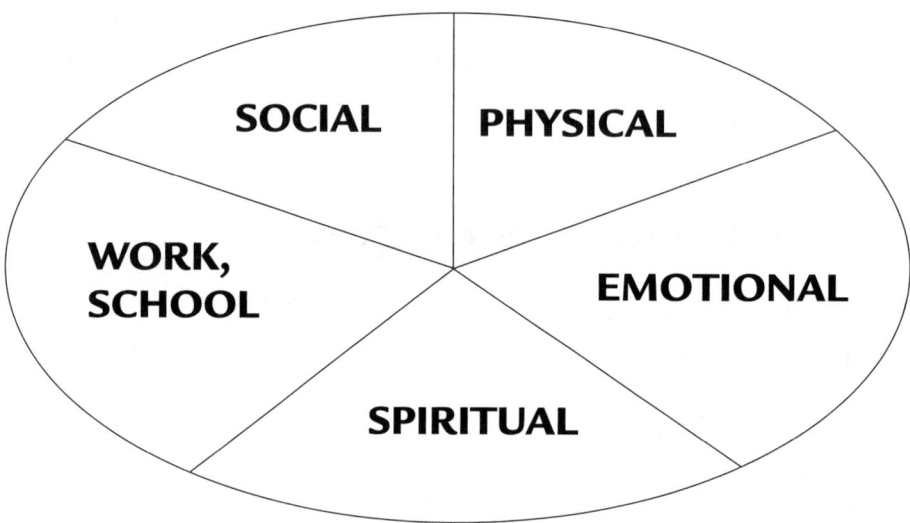

Exercise 9.3 Balance

1. Discuss with your group what might fit under each section of the wheel.

Discuss what the result might be if you took any area out.

2. Now, examine your own life. Score each of the areas below from 1 to 10, with 10 being the Very Best, 1 being the Worst or Poorest.

_____   Physical

_____   Emotional

_____   Social

_____   Work/School

_____   Spiritual

3. What can you do to improve the balance in your life?

_____

_____

_____

Your Moral Code

Did you know that all of your actions are guided by your moral codes? For example, if your moral code is that you do not do drugs, and you go to a friend's house where drugs are being used, the decision is much easier. You leave. But if you are unsure of your values, you might be going back and forth in your mind. Do I stay or do I go? Back and forth, you lean on your friends for advice. Not wanting to look stupid, or uncool, you can't say "no." So, you end up staying and get a hot urinalysis. Now, you are in trouble with your parole officer.

Values and moral codes are guides. Most of our moral codes are based on the Golden Rule: Do unto others as you would have them do unto you. This rule is present in some form in almost every religion and philosophy. If that concept were followed by all people, probably we would not need so many laws.

Alcoholics Anonymous (AA) and Narcotics Anonymous (NA) support groups have a step called "taking your moral inventory." Have you ever taken a moral inventory? What are the codes you live by? Who have you injured by your actions? What changes can you make in the future? These are just a few questions that you might consider as you examine your own moral codes.

"Self-Portrait" by DM. Media: Candy bar wrappers (Kit Kat, Hershey's with Almonds, M&M peanuts, Milky Way, Snickers, Butterfingers, Twix, Reese's), soda bottle wrappers (Diet Pepsi) and glue on Stonehenge. Courtesy of Art Behind Bars.

Exercise 9.4 What Are Your Values?

Do you know your values? Have you even thought of them?

Value Survey

A. Take a look at the following survey and list your values in order of importance, starting with #1. Be honest with yourself.

___	Happiness	___	A beautiful home
___	Family	___	Friendship
___	Sexual pleasure	___	Having fun
___	Fame	___	Self-respect
___	Spirituality	___	Freedom
___	Excitement	___	Wisdom
___	Money	___	Stimulating work

B. Now, take a few moments and discuss your choices with the group. How do you think these values determine choices you make in life?

_____

_____

_____

Spiritual and religious areas: One section of balance is the spiritual area. Some people think that spiritual means religious—having and following a particular religion. While religion can be a part of spirituality, spirituality includes much more. Have you ever asked yourself any of the following questions?

Who am I?
What is my purpose in life?
What is my place in the universe?

Asking yourself these questions is part of the journey to realizing your own spirituality. Why are you here? Can you help another person along the way? Can you use your experiences in life so far to help someone else? Do you have a purpose in life? People who have a purpose appear to be healthier and happier. Remember, everything is a matter of how you perceive it.

If you are incarcerated right now, it can seem very bleak and pointless. But perhaps someone in your own cell house can benefit from your experience. Spirituality also includes your ethics and moral code, as well as how you treat other people.

Religion often helps provide the answer to some of these questions. It can provide guidelines and instructions to help you as you move through life. It can provide hope and solace when you are sad and grieving. Certainly, it can be a very important part of your rehabilitation. Think about it. If you follow the Golden Rule, if you truly believe in treating your fellow beings with love and mercy, you would not be assaulting other people. You certainly would not assault your wife or partner.

Think about your own spiritual and religious beliefs. Where are you at this point in your life? Remember that finding your spirituality can be a journey. It is much like a quest and sometimes there are detours along the way. But continuing that journey is critical to your self-management.

Empathy and Compassion: Developing empathy and having compassion for other people is an important part of spirituality. It is also valuable in developing feelings for victims. If you cannot feel what your victims might be feeling, you just may continue with criminal behavior. You might "disconnect" from the victims and simply treat them as objects to be used to fulfill your own needs.

What is *empathy*? *The Random House Webster's College Dictionary* (2001) defines empathy as: "The identification with or vicarious experiencing of the feelings, thoughts, etc., of another." In other words, you can put yourself in the victim's shoes. Try to imagine what it would be like if someone beat up your mother or sister—or you. This can help you to understand just what empathy means.

It is often hard for a person to understand abuse from the victim's point of view. How do you feel when someone calls you a vulgar name? How do you feel when someone punches you in the face? Have you ever been sexually assaulted? If so, you might understand how someone who has been sexually assaulted might feel.

In other words, if you have had these experiences, then perhaps you can imagine how others might feel if they are verbally, physically, or sexually abused. But what if you have not had these experiences? It is still possible for you to imagine how these abuses would feel. You need to be able to do this because gaining empathy is a critical part of change. In other words, it is important to be able to relate the pain that your victim experiences, if you are going to stop abusing and victimizing others.

Hands Down: A Domestic Violence Treatment Workbook

In addition, empathy acts as a curb to keep you from going around beating up other people—physically or emotionally. If you understand and can experience the feelings of victims, then you may stop harming others. You do not like violence when it happens to you or people you love. Therefore, you can learn to stop and think about your behavior before you abuse others.

Compassion, on the other hand, is defined as: "A feeling of deep sympathy and sorrow for someone struck by misfortune, accompanied by a desire to alleviate the suffering." Compassion is caring. It is very close to empathy, but empathy is more like imagining yourself in another person's place. Compassion helps us to recognize the suffering of other people and to know that we, too, have similar feelings. As a result of compassion, you can develop the desire to help others when they are in need. For example, compassion has moved many people to help others left homeless or jobless by the hurricanes along the Gulf Coast. Recognizing how someone suffers emotional pain when abused by others can lead you to realize how important it is not to cause pain and suffering to others.

Both empathy and compassion can act as motivators for you to stop and examine your own values and responses to others. As a result, you may be able to make positive changes in your thinking and behavior. Without these two qualities, it can be very difficult to make healthy progress in relationships.

Exercise 9.5 Empathy

1. Describe a situation in which you have victimized another person. Were you able to feel empathy for that person? Did you victimize the person anyway? Be prepared to discuss how this has affected you and the other person.

_____

_____

_____

_____

2. When was the last time you felt compassion for another human being? Describe the feeling and any action you took as a result.

_____
_____
_____
_____

3. Where do you see your feelings of compassion and empathy today? How do you think you could improve them?

_____
_____
_____
_____

Relapse Prevention

When you think of relapse prevention, you may think of drug and alcohol treatment. Of course, relapse prevention is extremely important in preventing a return to substance abuse. If you used substances when committing any act of violence, you should know how important it is to prevent a return to those old behaviors. And you probably have heard of the saying, "One day at a time." This saying refers to one way that addicts continue to remain clean and sober.

However, relapse prevention also can refer to any type of behavior or addiction. For example, people who are gambling addicts struggle with controlling their behaviors and habits continually. In fact, some of those people actually may experience a "high," when they win at gambling. But have you noticed that some people who win the lottery continue to gamble. It is not the money that drives them. It is a chemical feeling of pleasure—a "high" much like shooting up a drug. And, just like alcoholics, they, too, can experience relapse by returning to their old behaviors.

Remember that one definition of addiction is **continuing the same behavior over and over again with negative, even destructive, results.**

Therefore, people who have been in the habit of using violence toward other people might also be said to be addicted to that type of behavior. Perhaps you may be one of those individuals. If so, it is extremely important that you continually examine your own behavior and check for warning signs of relapse. If you fail to recognize the warning signs and revert back to your old behaviors, then you may produce more victims. And, one critical goal of this course is **no more victims**.

There are warning signs or cues that will provide you with an opportunity to stop and think about your feelings and options, so that you do not relapse. People who relapse do not suddenly become high, drunk, or abusive. Most people experience warning signs that cause them to return to self-medicating with substances or other behaviors.

The following list may help as you continue on your journey toward nonaddictive and nonviolent behavior. Read the list carefully and review each area with your group. Be prepared to discuss what the signs mean to you and share examples.

Relapse Signs

- **Change.** Remember any type of change can produce stress and trigger a response. A death, a separation, a job change, a newborn child—these are but a few examples of change. Even change that seems positive, such as the newborn child, can produce stress. Be alert to change. Remember external events, such as terrorists' attacks, floods, or earthquakes, also can cause change within you and trigger a response. Even such events as feelings of loneliness, shame, guilt, or anger can cause a slip or relapse back into your old habits.

- **Stress.** Along with change, greater levels of stress can make you overreact to situations. When you experience trouble at work, legal problems, a spouse who cheats on you—all of these contribute to stress and health problems. Of course, if you experience more of these problems at once, the greater the stress level. This "bad" or negative stress can block your thinking so that you make lousy decisions. You may find yourself resorting to distorted thinking. Some of that thinking may be: "What the hell? It doesn't make any difference anyway. I'll just have one little drink."

- **Denial.** As your stress levels go up, you may start denying the stress and pressure, blaming others and life situations for your problems. "I'm okay," you may tell yourself. "It's not a big deal." "I'm a man; I can handle it." If you do not communicate your frustrations or anger to others, your denial can lead to your making bad choices. This can lead to arguing and domestic violence.

- **Thought Changes.** Beware of changes in your thinking—negative thoughts, blaming others, or distorted events. Thoughts like, "I never get a break." "She must be sleeping around." "No one is going to talk to me like that." "I should be able to control my family." This type of thinking can set you right back on a destructive track.

- **Feeling Tension and Arguing.** As your stress level rises and as your thinking becomes more distorted, you may become more argumentative. You may begin "nitpicking" with your partner, finding more and more fault with her behaviors. The tension continues to grow, becoming more frequent and severe, and now you may find yourself falling back into the old cycles of violence.

- **Judgment Lapse.** You find yourself throwing caution away. You tell yourself that everyone has arguments, so what if we are quarreling. So what if the neighbors can hear us. It is nobody's business but ours. Yes, you know you could get arrested again or your partner might leave you, but you begin to develop an attitude that says "What the hell? It doesn't matter."

- **Return to Drinking/Drugging.** This occurs as stress builds and your judgment lapses. Since you are not using tools such as healthy communication, timeouts, meditation, or other stress-relievers, you turn to substances to cope with your situation. You rationalize this by saying to yourself, "It's okay. Just this one drink, fix, or drag—it'll help me relax."

- **Relapse.** You lose control. If you are truly an addict, you most probably will not stop with the lapse in judgment. Probably you will continue to drink or use. You no longer make rational decisions and come to believe that everything you learned is "stupid." With full relapse, you eventually may develop physical problems, such as stomach ulcers or cirrhosis of the liver. Or, you may become depressed. You also could end up assaulting your partner and possibly getting locked up.

Remember that the sooner you intervene or stop the relapse cycle, the easier it will be to remain violence free!

Other Contributing Factors

Many factors contribute to whether a person remains sober or clean or whether they remain violence free. Relapse is caused by a combination of feelings and events. Some of the other factors you may want to consider on your journey to a violence-free life include:

- Hanging around old places and old friends, what are known as *slippery places*
- Stopping any prescribed medications without doctor's orders, especially medications used for anxiety, stress, depression, and so forth
- Keeping alcohol, drugs, or equipment used to "get high" around the house
- Changing patterns in eating, sleeping, or personal habits
- Isolating yourself, not using a support system, whether AA/NA, family friends, clergy, or others
- Feeling overconfident, that you do not need help with problems or feelings
- Not getting help when you become stressed or worried
- Feeling constantly bored, irritable, or angry
- Avoiding or refusing to deal with problems
- Engaging in any obsessive behavior, such as overeating, gambling, working all the time, sexual excess
- Ignoring relapse warning signs and triggers

Exercise 9.6 Relapse Prevention Warning Signs

1. Examine your past history of any substance abuse or violent behaviors. In the past, what have been your warning signs or cues? What situations or events have triggered relapses for you? Discuss these with your group.

_____
_____
_____
_____
_____

2. What do you think you can do in the future to prevent relapsing into the same behavior?

_____
_____
_____
_____
_____

Prevention Techniques

What can you do in those early stages to prevent yourself from going back to violent behavior?

1. **Communication.** Remember Chapter 5: Communication? Review it. To avoid relapse, you need to talk with your partner, your support systems, and your sponsor, if you have one. Be honest about your fears. Share your feelings with them.

2. **Use your support system.** If you are in AA or NA, stay active. If you have a church family, use that support system. People who do not have support systems tend to "fall apart" much more quickly when stress comes along.

3. **Use stress-management techniques** you learned in this workbook including exercising, developing hobbies and talents, relaxing, meditating, and praying.

4. **Ask for help.** This goes back to communication and your support group and is critical. Do not be afraid to ask for help when you are getting stressed and scared. Everybody has these feelings at times. Reach out and you will find a world of support. But if you sit around alone and feel sorry for yourself, no one will know, so no one will help you.

5. **Review your anger-management techniques.** Remember, anger is a secondary emotion and usually is driven by fear. Work with your fears. You cannot deal with them until you turn around and face them. Be honest with yourself.

6. **Watch for denial.** If your partner (or anyone else) accuses you of denial, believe them. Refusing to acknowledge denial can lead you straight to relapse.

7. **Continue to work on your spiritual path.** Do something for someone else. It is amazing how your focus can change when you quit thinking about yourself all the time.

8. **Review any situations that have produced triggers.** Write them down. Talk about them with your partner. How can you eliminate them or change the outcome? Discuss this when you are both feeling loving and calm.

9. **Seek counseling or guidance.** You may want to enroll in another domestic violence or anger management program. Or, you may seek some couple's counseling. Perhaps you can seek out a clergyperson for support and guidance.

10. **Journal.** Write down the things that are bothering you. This can act as a way to work out your frustrations and also help you to figure out how to handle your problems.

11. **Make a list of all of the things you have been doing right.** Post them on your refrigerator or in another prominent spot. Read them over daily and remind yourself that you can live a nonviolent life.

Domestic Violence Prevention Plan

Take some time and think carefully about your past history and how you can change your future. As a final step toward completing this program, answer the following questions and share your answers with your group.

Name _____

1. Write about one past domestic episode, especially one in which you were arrested or the victim was injured in some way. Be very specific.

_____
_____
_____
_____

2. What can you do to be sure that this will never happen again? Be very detailed. Look at triggers, cues, stress, your own thinking process, and so forth.

_____
_____
_____
_____

3. Are you still in contact with this victim? Describe your current relationship with her.

_____
_____
_____
_____

4. Did you ever make amends or try to? Tell the result.

5. Name one trigger that pushed your buttons with this person? Explain why you think this was a hot spot for you.

6. Would this trigger still set you off? Why or why not?

7. Write a single page describing how you think you have changed. Cover the key parts of this program in your page and describe any progress that you believe you have made.

Conclusion

Throughout this workbook, you have heard and read the word "choices" many times. You can sit through months of domestic violence classes. You can practice skills in a classroom setting. You can mouth all the right words and act like you really have learned something, as if you have turned over a new leaf. You are now a new man. But when you look yourself in the mirror, when you take off your mask, who are you really?

Only you are in charge of your choices in life. "You control your destiny." Only you can decide whether you want to go on offending, being a violent man, and emotionally, physically, and/or sexually assaulting your partner. That is up to you. However, this workbook can act as a guide for you.

Not all the answers are inside these pages. When you face the real world, with real problems and your own raw feelings, you may find it difficult to remain violence free. Change is not easy. But with these tools, you will have a foundation and can become a nonviolent role model for others—including your children.

Other people are watching you. If you want to see change around you, if you want your wife and children to act differently, then you must set the example. You can continue to live in violence, rage, anger, and with lies. You can live on the edge or in chaos. And you can continue your journey toward prison or death. On the other hand, you can change your life, manage your stress, and become more self-confident, hopeful, and peaceful. You can find happiness. Only you can make the choice. We wish you well!

"Parrot Sunset" by BN. Media: Acrylic on canvas. Courtesy of Art Behind Bars.

Additional Resources and Reading

Aasved, Mikal J. 2002. *The Psychodynamics and Psychology of Gambling: The Gambler's Mind (Gambling Theory and Research Series, Vol. 1)*. Springfield, Illinois: Charles C. Thomas Publishers.

Albom, Mitch. 2003. *The Five People You Meet in Heaven*. New York: Hyperion Books.

Allen, Marvin with Jo Robinson. 1993. *Angry Men, Passive Men*. New York: Fawcett Columbine.

American Psychological Association. 1996. *Violence and the Family: Report of the APA Presidential Task Force on Violence and the Family*. Washington, D.C.: American Psychological Association.

Amherst H. Wilder Foundation. 1995. *On the Level: Foundations for Violence-free Living*. St. Paul, Minnesota: Amherset H. Wilder Foundation.

Bernstein, Douglas A., Alison Clarke-Stewart, Edward J. Roy, Thomas K. Srull, and Christopher D. Wickens. 1994. *Psychology, 3rd Ed*. Boston: Houghton Mifflin Co.

Berry, Dawn Bradley. 2000. *The Domestic Violence Sourcebook*. New York: McGraw Hill.

Bureau of Justice Statistics. 2001. *Special Report: Intimate Partner Violence and Age of Victim, 1993–1999*. Washington, D.C.: Bureau of Justice Statistics.

Bureau of Justice Statistics. February 2003. *Crime Data Brief, Intimate Partner Violence, 1993–2001*. Washington, D.C.: Bureau of Justice Statistics.

Carlson, B. E. 2000. Children Exposed to Intimate Partner Violence: Research Findings and Implications for Intervention. *Trauma, Violence and Abuse*. 1(4): 321-340.

Centers for Disease Control and Prevention and the National Institute of Justice. July 2000. *Extent, Nature, and Consequences of Intimate Partner Violence*. Washington, D.C.: National Institute of Justice.

Centers for Disease Control and Prevention. April 2003. *Costs of Intimate Partner Violence against Women in the United States*. Atlanta: Centers for Disease Control and Prevention.

Centers for Disease Control and Prevention. 2005. *CDC Study Documents High Costs and Impact of Intimate Partner Violence*. (Oct. 25, 2005). Centers for Disease Control and Prevention, www.cdc.gov

Clark, Lynn. 2002. *SOS Help for Emotions, 2nd Ed*. Bowling Green, Kentucky: SOS Program and Parents Press.

Commonwealth Fund. May 1999. *Health Concerns across a Woman's Lifespan: 1998 Survey of Women's Health*. New York: The Commonwealth Fund.

Cullen, Murray. 1992. *Cage Your Rage: An Inmate's Guide to Anger Control*. Alexandria, Virginia: American Correctional Association.

Cullen, Murray and Robert E. Freeman-Longo. 1994. *Men and Anger*. Brandon, Vermont: Safer Society Press.

Cullen, Murray and Sandra Piekarski. 2002. *TRY: Treatment Readiness for You: A Workbook for Abusers in Relationships*. Alexandria, Virginia: American Correctional Association.

Domestic Violence: Protecting Yourself and Your Children. May 2005, www.familydoctor.org.

Dutton, D. 1994. The Dynamics of Domestic Violence: Understanding the Response from Battered Women. *Florida Bar Journal*. 68(9): 24, 26.

———. 1994. Post-Traumatic Stress Disorder among Battered Women: Analysis of Legal Implications. *Behavioral Science and the Law*. 12: 215, 219.

———. 1995. *The Batterer: A Psychological Profile*. New York: Basic Books.

———. 1998. *The Abusive Personality: Violence and Control in Intimate Relationships*. New York: Guilford.

Edleson, J. L. 1999. The Overlap between Child Maltreatment and Woman Battering. *Violence Against Women*. 5(2): 134–154.

Ellis, Albert and Raymond Chip Tafrate 1998. *How to Control Your Anger Before It Controls You*. Secaucus, New Jersey: Carol Publishing.

Engel, Beverly. 2002. *The Emotionally Abusive Relationship*. Hoboken, New Jersey: John Wiley and Sons.

Evans, Patricia. 1992. *The Verbally Abusive Relationship*. Holbrook, Massachusetts: Bob Adams, Inc.

Gaffney, Linda. 2006. *My Daddy Does Good Things, Too! A Book for (and about) Children of Incarcerated Parents*. Olympia, Washington: Homeplace Press.

Gazmararian, J. A., R. Petersen, A. M. Spitz, M. M. Goodwin, L. E. Saltzman, and J. S. Marks. 2000. Violence and Reproductive Health: Current Knowledge and Future Research Directions. *Maternal and Child Health Journal*. 4(2): 79–84.

Geffner, Robert, Peter, G. Jaffe, and Marlies Sundermann, eds. 2000. *Children Exposed to Domestic Violence: Current Issues in Research, Intervention, Prevention and Policy Development.* Binghamton, New York: Haworth Press.

Gondolf, Edward W. and David M. Russell. 1987. *Man to Man: A Guide for Men in Abusive Relationships.* New York: Sulzburger Graham Publishing.

Graham-Bermann, Sandra A. and Jeffrey L. Edleson, eds. 2001. *Domestic Violence in the Lives of Children: The Future of Research Intervention and Social Policy.* Washington, D.C.: American Psychological Association.

Hamberger, L. Kevin and Claire Renzetti, eds. 1996. *Domestic Partner Abuse.* New York: Springer.

Ingraham, Linda, Steve Bell, and Ned Rollo. 1991. *Life Without a Crutch.* Garland, Texas: Open Inc.

Jacobs, Ed and Nina Spadaro. 2003. *Leading Groups in Corrections: Skills and Techniques.* Alexandria, Virginia: American Correctional Association.

Jillson, Irene Anne and Bettina Scott. 1996. *Violence, Women and Alcohol: Reducing the Risks, Redressing the Consequences.* Washington, D.C.: Department of Health and Human Services, Draft Report.

Lindsay, Michael, Robert W. McBride, and Constance M. Platt. 1999. *Change Is the Third Path: A Workbook for Ending Abusive and Violent Behavior.* Littleton, Colorado: Gylantic Publishing.

National Clearinghouse on Child Abuse and Neglect Information (DHHS). 2003. *Children and Domestic Violence: A Bulletin for Professionals,* http://www.nccanch.acf.hhs.gov/pubs/factsheets/domesticviolence.cfm.

National Coalition Against Domestic Violence (NCADV) Public Policy Office, www.ncadv.org.

Paymar, Michael. 1993. *Violent No More: Helping Men End Domestic Abuse.* Alameda, California: Hunter House.

Pearson, Patricia. 1997. *When She Was Bad.* New York: Viking Press.

Peled, Inat, Peter G. Jaffe, and Jeffrey L. Edleson. 1995. *Ending the Cycle of Violence: Community Responses to Children of Battered Women.* Thousand Oaks, California: Sage Publications.

Pelzer, David. 1995. *A Child Called It.* Deerfield Beach, Florida: Health Communications, Inc.

Pence, Ellen and Michael Paymar. 1993. *Education Groups for Men Who Batter: The Duluth Model.* New York: Springer.

Potter-Efron, Ron and Pat Potter-Efron. 1995. *Letting Go of Anger.* Oakland, California: New Harbinger Publications.

Rollo, Ned. 2002. *99 Days and a Get Up: A Guide to Success Following Release for Inmates and Their Loved Ones, 3rd Ed.* Garland, Texas: Open Inc.

Ruden, Ronald A. and Marcia Byaleck. 2000. *The Craving Brain.* New York: HarperCollins.

Schechter, S. and J. Edleson. 2000. *Domestic Violence and Children: Creating a Public Response.* New York: Center on Crime, Communities and Culture for the Open Society Institute.

Sedgwick County, Kansas, Office of District Attorney. *Myths and Facts about Domestic Violence,* www.sedgwickcounty.org/da/dv_facts.html.

Silverman, Jay G., Anita Raj, Lorelei A. Mucci, and Jeanne E. Hathaway. 2001. Dating Violence against Adolescent Girls and Associated Substance Use, Unhealthy Weight Control, Sexual Risk Behavior, Pregnancy, and Suicidality. *Journal of the American Medical Association*. 286 (5).

Sonkin, D. J. and M. Durphy. 1982. *Learning to Live Without Violence: A Handbook for Men*. San Francisco: Volcano Press.

Sonkin, D. J., Del Martin, and Lenore E. A. Walker. 1985. *The Male Batterer: A Treatment Approach*. New York: Springer.

Stawar, Terry L. 2007. *How to Be a Responsible Father: A Workbook for Offenders*. Alexandria, Virginia: American Correctional Association.

Strong, Bryan, Christine DeVault, and Barbara W. Sayad. 1998. *The Marriage and Family Experience*. Belmont, California: Wadsworth Publishing Co.

Tjaden, Patricia and Nancy Thoennes. 2000. *Extent, Nature, and Consequences of Intimate Partner Violence*. Washington, D.C.: National Institute of Justice.

U.S. Department of Justice. March 1998. *Violence by Intimates: Analysis of Data of Crimes by Current or Former Spouses, Boyfriends, and Girlfriends*. Washington, D.C.: U.S. Department of Justice.

Urquhart, Judith and Murray Cullen. 2003. *Cage Your Rage for Women*. Alexandria, Virginia: American Correctional Association.

Walker, Lenore. 1984. *The Battered Woman Syndrome*. New York: Springer.

Walker, Lenore. 1994. *Abused Women and Survivor Therapy*. Washington, D.C.: American Psychological Association.

Wegscheider-Cruse, Sharon. 1989. *Another Chance: Hope and Health for the Alcoholic Family, 2nd Ed*. Palo Alto, California: Science and Behavior Books, Inc.

Wekerle, Christine and Anne Marie Wall. 2002. *The Violence and Addiction Equation: Theoretical and Clinical Issues in Substance Abuse and Relationship Violence*. E. Sussex, Britain: Brunner-Routledge Publishers.

Wexler, David B. 2000. *Domestic Violence 2000*. New York: W.W. Norton and Co.